Uncle Ben's®

The Magic of Rice
COOKBOOK

A Benjamin Company/Rutledge Book

SBN 87502-004-6
Copyright © 1969 by Uncle Ben's, Inc.
The new supermarket edition prepared
and produced by Rutledge Books.
Published by The Supermarket Book Company.
For further information, contact
The Benjamin Company, Inc.
485 Madison Avenue
New York, N.Y. 10017
Library of Congress Catalog Card Number 70-92095
Printed in the United States of America

Contents

TO WHET THE APPETITE

Easy-make, easy-cook appetizers

NIPPY CHEESE-RICE COCKTAIL BALLS

18 to 20 appetizers

1 cup Uncle Ben's®
   Quick Rice
1 cup water
½ teaspoon salt
½ teaspoon butter
   or margarine
2 cups sharp Cheddar
   cheese
1 egg white, beaten

1½ tablespoons
   prepared mustard
1 teaspoon prepared
   horseradish
¼ teaspoon cayenne
Fat for deep frying
¼ cup flour
1 tablespoon paprika

Combine rice, water, salt and butter in a saucepan. Bring to a boil, cover, lower heat and cook until all liquid is absorbed. Remove from heat and set in a pan of cold tap water to cool quickly—about 15 minutes. Mash rice, cheese, egg white and seasonings together with a fork until well blended. Form into 1-inch balls, roll in a mixture of flour and paprika. Chill 1 hour or more. Fry in deep fat at 375° F. until golden brown.

PERINO'S WILD RICE MUSHROOMS

12 to 16 servings

1 cup chopped
   onions
3 tablespoons butter
   or margarine
2½ cups chicken broth
1 package (6 ounces)
   Uncle Ben's®
   Long Grain &
   Wild Rice
½ cup minced cooked
   ham

3 cloves garlic,
   minced
½ cup butter
4 dozen 2-inch-
   diameter fresh
   mushrooms,
   stems removed
2 tablespoons lemon
   juice
Salt, pepper

Cook onions in 3 tablespoons melted butter until soft. Stir in broth, ham, rice, packet of seasonings. Bring to boil. Cover; cook over moderate heat until water is absorbed, about 25 minutes. Meanwhile cook garlic in ½ cup butter until golden; add mushrooms and lemon juice. Cook over moderate heat 4 to 5 minutes, turning mushrooms once. Drain. Sprinkle with salt and pepper. Mound rice mixture into mushrooms. Serve hot.

You'll want to know: These stuffed mushrooms are a specialty of Perino's restaurant in Los Angeles.

STUFFED PEPPER APPETIZERS   12 servings

⅔ cup finely chopped
  onions
2 cloves garlic,
  minced
2 tablespoons olive
  oil
3 cups chicken broth
1¼ cups Uncle Ben's®
  Converted® Rice

2 teaspoons seasoned
  salt
⅛ teaspoon powdered
  saffron
6 medium green
  peppers
Water
Paprika
Anchovy fillets

Cook onions and garlic in olive oil until browned. Add chicken broth and bring to boil. Stir in rice and seasoned salt. Cover tightly and cook over low heat 15 minutes. Stir in saffron and continue cooking until water is absorbed—about 10 minutes more. Cut stems out of green peppers; remove seeds. Cut thin slice off bottoms to level. Stuff rice mixture firmly into peppers. Put in heavy casserole or Dutch oven with cover. Add water to ½-inch depth. Cover and bring to simmer over medium heat. Cook 10 to 15 minutes or until peppers are soft but still crisp. Chill. Cut in half lengthwise and garnish each half with a sprinkling of paprika and an anchovy fillet.

You'll want to know: These stuffed peppers are served at Chez Paul, one of Chicago's great restaurants.

6

Right, Nippy Cheese-Rice Cocktail Balls, Wild Rice Stuffed Mushrooms, Stuffed Peppers

BRIGHT BEGINNINGS

Hearty, taste-like-more soups

CREAM OF TURKEY SOUP
4 servings

2½ cups stock or
 bouillon
¼ cup flour
¼ cup butter or
 margarine
½ cup light cream
1 teaspoon celery salt
½ teaspoon salt
½ teaspoon monoso-
 dium glutamate

¼ teaspoon white
 pepper
½ teaspoon crushed
 sweet basil or
 marjoram
1 cup cooked Uncle
 Ben's® Con-
 verted® Rice
½ cup finely chopped
 cooked turkey

Prepare stock by simmering leftover carcass of turkey in water 45 minutes or by dissolving 3 chicken bouillon cubes in 2½ cups boiling water. Blend flour with melted butter or margarine. Slowly add stock and cook over low heat until thin sauce results. Stir in cream and seasonings. Add rice and turkey and heat thoroughly. Garnish with finely chopped celery tops, parsley or croutons.

SOPA OPORTO
4 servings

Here's a Portuguese rice soup, made all the more
tasty by the addition of rich-flavored port wine

4 cups chicken stock
 or broth
¼ cup Uncle Ben's®
 Converted® Rice
Salt, pepper

2 egg yolks
4 tablespoons heavy
 cream
2 tablespoons port
 wine

8

Bring chicken stock to a boil. Add rice and simmer for 20 to 25 minutes or until rice is tender. Season to taste with salt and pepper. Beat egg yolks with cream and port; very gradually stir into hot soup. Heat through, but do not boil.

Another way: Substitute lemon juice for the port and what do you have? Greek Avgolemono Soup—equally delicious.

BRUNSWICK SOUP
8 to 10 servings

2 quarts chicken stock
1 cup sliced celery
1 cup sliced carrots
12 to 15 whole small onions
2 cups green peas
1 package (10 ounces) frozen okra
3 cups canned tomatoes
2 tablespoons sugar
1 tablespoon salt
½ teaspoon pepper
1 can whole kernel corn
2 cups Uncle Ben's® Quick Rice

Combine all ingredients, except corn and rice, and simmer about 30 minutes or until vegetables are tender. Add corn and rice. Simmer until rice is tender—about 6 or 7 minutes.

Quick Trick: Leftover rice? "Hash" it with canned corned beef, a bit of chopped onion. Use a bouillon cube dissolved in hot water to moisten; heat gently.

SHRIMP GUMBO

5 to 6 servings

1 cup Uncle Ben's®
   Converted® Rice
2 cups sliced fresh
   okra
⅓ cup fat or bacon
   drippings
⅔ cup chopped green
   onions and tops
3 cloves garlic, finely
   chopped
1½ teaspoons salt
2 teaspoons black
   pepper
2 pounds shrimp,
   shelled, deveined
2 cups hot water
1 cup stewed
   tomatoes
2 whole bay leaves
6 drops hot pepper
   sauce

Cook rice according to package directions. Meanwhile sauté okra in fat, stirring constantly, about 10 minutes or until okra appears dry. Add onion, garlic, salt, pepper and shrimp. Cook about 5 minutes. Add water, tomatoes and bay leaves. Cover and simmer 20 minutes. Remove bay leaves. Add hot pepper sauce. Spoon over rice and serve.

CHICKEN GUMBO WITH RICE

6 to 8 servings

1 large stewing chicken,
   cut up
Salt, pepper
2 tablespoons butter
   or margarine
1 cup diced ham
1 small onion, minced
1 green pepper,
   chopped
1 sprig thyme or
   parsley, minced
6 fresh or 1½ cups
   canned tomatoes
1 cup sliced okra
2 quarts boiling water
4 cups hot cooked
   Uncle Ben's®
   Converted® Rice

Cut up the chicken as for stewing. Season chicken with salt and pepper. Heat butter in soup kettle. Add chicken and ham; cover tightly. Simmer 10 minutes. Add onion, pepper and thyme, and brown. Add tomatoes, sliced okra and boiling water; simmer 2 hours or until done. Bone chicken and return meat to soup. Serve in a tureen. Accompany with a bowl of cooked rice or serve in bowls with a generous mound of rice.

11

Left, Shrimp Gumbo

FEATURE ATTRACTION: MEAT

New ways with old favorites

PEACHY LAMB CHOPS

Deliciously glazed lamb chops, each one
topped with its own tasty peach garnish

4 shoulder lamb chops,
 cut ¾-inch thick
1 tablespoon shortening
4 teaspoons chopped
 onion
2 tablespoons brown
 sugar
2 tablespoons prepared
 mustard

1 teaspoon Worcester-
 shire sauce
1 package Uncle Ben's®
 Long Grain & Wild
 Rice
4 green pepper rings
4 canned peach halves

Slash edges of fat on chops. Brown in shortening on
both sides. Sprinkle with salt. Place in a baking dish.
Sprinkle with onion. Cover and bake in a 350° F. oven
20 minutes. Combine sugar, mustard, Worcestershire.
Uncover chops. Spread with half of brown sugar mixture. Bake, uncovered, 20 minutes longer. Cook rice
according to package directions. Brush chops with
remaining brown sugar mixture. Top each chop with
a green pepper ring and center a peach half in each
ring. Bake 10 minutes longer. Turn out rice on warm
platter. Top with chops.

PORK CHOPS, GOLDEN RICE

6 servings

6 pork chops, cut
 ¾-inch thick

½ teaspoon salt
2 tablespoons oil

½ cup chopped onion
1 cup Uncle Ben's®
   Converted® Rice
2 chicken bouillon
   cubes
½ teaspoon turmeric
   or curry

2½ cups boiling water
½ cup sour cream
2 tablespoons
   chopped parsley

Slash fat on edges of chops with knife; sprinkle chops with salt. Slowly brown in oil, pour off excess fat. Add onion, rice. Dissolve bouillon cubes and turmeric in water and add. Cover and cook slowly over low heat about 30 to 40 minutes, until chops are tender and liquid is absorbed. Remove chops to warm platter, piling at one end. Stir sour cream into rice mixture. Cook over low heat until heated through. Pile on other half of platter. Sprinkle with parsley.

KENTUCKY PORK-AND-APPLE RICE
4 to 5 servings

2 cans (12 ounces
   each) apple juice
1 cup water
1 cup Uncle Ben's®
   Converted® Rice
1 teaspoon salt
1 medium apple,
   chopped

1½ pounds boneless
   lean pork roast
Flour, salt, pepper
¼ cup cooking oil or
   fat
1 beef bouillon cube
2 teaspoons instant-
   minced onion

Bring 1 can apple juice and the water to a boil in a saucepan. Stir in rice and salt. Cover tightly and cook over low heat until all liquid is absorbed, about 25 minutes. Stir in apple. Meanwhile cut pork into thin strips. Coat with flour seasoned with salt and pepper. Brown in hot oil. Add 1 can apple juice, onion and bouillon cube. Cover and simmer over moderate heat 15 minutes, or until done. Serve pork with apple rice.   13

SHISH KEBAB, QUICK PILAF   4 servings

1½ pounds tender lamb
½ cup red wine
¼ cup oil
1 onion, diced
1 clove garlic, minced
Salt, pepper, oregano
3 green peppers, cut
    in chunks
3 tomatoes, cut in
    quarters

12 mushroom caps
    (reserve stems)
2 tablespoons butter
    or margarine
¼ cup chopped onion
2 cups Uncle Ben's®
    Quick Rice
1⅔ cups water

Cut lamb into 1½-inch cubes. Combine wine, oil, onion, garlic and seasonings; pour over lamb. Marinate at room temperature 2 hours, or overnight in the refrigerator. Fill 4 skewers alternately with meat, pepper chunks, tomato wedges and mushrooms. Brush with marinade. Broil quickly, close to heat, until done to taste. Serve on bed of Quick Pilaf.

Quick Pilaf: Melt butter; cook chopped onion, chopped mushroom stems a few minutes. Add rice, stir until golden. Add water, bring to boil, cover, simmer 5 minutes.

LAMB CURRY WITH RICE   6 servings

1 cup Uncle Ben's®
    Converted® Rice
1 cup sliced, peeled
    onions
¼ cup diced green
    pepper
1 cup diced celery
1 clove garlic,
    minced
4 tablespoons fat or
    oil

3 cups diced cooked
    lamb
1 teaspoon curry
    powder (more, if
    desired)
1½ teaspoons salt
1 tablespoon Wor-
    cestershire sauce
2 cups lamb gravy
    or stock

14   Cook rice according to package directions; keep hot.

Above, Shish Kebab; below, Lamb Curry with Rice

Cook onion, green pepper, celery, garlic in fat. Add remaining ingredients. Cover; cook about 30 minutes over low heat. (If stock is used, thicken with 2 tablespoons flour blended with ¼ cup cold water.) Serve in border of cooked rice with chutney.

FESTIVAL PORK CHOPS   4 servings

2 cups cooked Uncle
  Ben's® Con-
  verted® Rice
4 lean pork chops
1 tablespoon fat
¼ cup diced onion
⅓ cup diced celery
2 tablespoons diced
  green pepper

1½ cups canned
  tomatoes
1½ teaspoons salt
¼ teaspoon pepper
2 tablespoons
  minced parsley

Brown chops in heavy skillet. Remove chops and add onion, celery and green pepper to drippings. Sauté until tender. Add tomatoes, salt, pepper. Simmer 10 minutes. Place chops in baking dish and sprinkle with salt and pepper. Top each chop with mound of ½ cup cooked rice. Pour sauce over all and sprinkle with parsley. Cover and bake in 350° F. oven for approximately 1 hour. Just before serving, spoon sauce from dish over chops.

CHINESE RICE WITH PORK   8 servings

¼ cup butter or
  margarine
1 pound pork, cut in
  ½-inch cubes
1 onion, sliced
½ cup sliced celery
1 tablespoon soy
  sauce

1 cup Uncle Ben's®
  Converted® Rice
1 teaspoon salt
3 cups chicken broth
½ cup sliced stuffed
  olives
¼ cup slivered,
  blanched almonds

Melt butter or margarine in a skillet over medium heat. Add pork and onion, brown well. Add celery, soy sauce, rice, salt, broth and sliced olives. Cover tightly. Cook over high heat until steaming freely, then turn heat to simmer and cook for 25 minutes. Garnish with slivered almonds before serving.

CANTONESE RICE

5 servings

1 cup Uncle Ben's®
   Converted® Rice
½ cup blanched
   almonds, slivered
1 tablespoon cooking
   oil
¾ cup (more or less)
   finely diced
   cooked ham

2 tablespoons raisins,
   minced
2 tablespoons
   chopped scallions
2 tablespoons soy
   sauce

Cook rice according to package directions. About 10 minutes before rice is ready, heat oil in heavy skillet. Add almonds and toast lightly, stirring frequently. Add ham, raisins and scallions. Stir for 2 minutes. Add soy sauce and cooked rice and toss gently with spoon until all ingredients are combined. Remove from heat and keep covered several minutes to blend flavors, or place in buttered casserole and hold in warm oven.

You'll want to know: Fresh orange slices make a surprising but just-right garnish for this dish. Serve with additional soy sauce if desired.

Quick Trick: Leftover rice? Combine it with a little chopped celery and onion and any leftover cooked vegetable in your refrigerator. Toss lightly with bottled French dressing or with oil and vinegar. Season to taste. Lunch is on, featuring Instant Rice Salad.

17

Above, Hawaiian Rice; below, Sukiyaki Skillet

HAWAIIAN RICE

5 to 6 servings

1½ pounds cubed lean
pork
3 tablespoons soy
sauce
½ cup pineapple juice
1 tablespoon vinegar
¾ teaspoon salt
½ teaspoon black
pepper
¼ teaspoon
powdered ginger

1 cup Uncle Ben's®
Converted® Rice
¾ cup diced green
peppers
1 tablespoon
cornstarch
1½ tablespoons water
1 cup (13½-ounce
can) pineapple
tidbits, drained

Combine pork, soy sauce, pineapple juice, vinegar, salt, black pepper and ginger in saucepan. Cook over low heat 1 hour or until pork is tender. Meanwhile cook rice according to package directions. When meat is tender, add green peppers and cook 7 minutes. Dissolve cornstarch in water and add to meat mixture, stirring constantly until thickened. Stir in pineapple tidbits and cooked rice. Garnish with salted peanuts and tomato slices. Serve hot.

SUKIYAKI SKILLET

8 servings

1 pound boneless
beef for stew
2 tablespoons oil
2 medium onions,
sliced
1 cup Uncle Ben's®
Converted® Rice
3 cups water
2½ teaspoons salt
1 small can mush-
rooms (stems
and pieces)
1 large green pepper,
cut in large cubes

5 to 6 large stalks
celery, cut in
1-inch pieces
1 can (1 pound)
bean sprouts
1 package (10
ounces) frozen
chopped
spinach, almost
thawed
3 tablespoons soy
sauce
1 tablespoon sugar

19

Cut stew meat into thin slices. Brown meat and onions in oil in a large skillet. Cover and cook slowly about 10 minutes. Add rice, water, salt and mushrooms with their liquid. Cover and cook slowly until rice is tender, about 25 minutes. Add pepper, celery, bean sprouts, spinach, soy sauce and sugar. Cover and cook until spinach is tender, 5 to 8 minutes. Do not overcook; vegetables should be crisp. Toss lightly to mix ingredients. Serve with extra soy sauce if desired.

Other ways: Pork may be substituted for beef—be sure it is well cooked. Water chestnuts may be added for crisp texture. Fresh spinach may be substituted for frozen.

JAMBALAYA RICE   4 to 6 servings

Fresh pork and ham make a fine flavor
combination in this tasty rice dish

¾ *pound fresh pork*
½ *cup finely chopped*
  onion
1 *finely chopped*
  garlic clove
3 *tablespoons fat*
1 *cup diced lean ham*
¼ *teaspoon thyme*
2 *tablespoons*
  chopped parsley

1 *bay leaf, broken*
  into pieces
4 *cups bouillon*
½ *teaspoon chili*
  powder
¼ *teaspoon salt*
Dash cayenne
1½ *cups Uncle Ben's®*
  Converted® Rice

Remove all fat from pork and cut into ½-inch cubes. Sauté onion, garlic and pork in fat until delicate brown. Add ham to pork mixture with thyme, parsley and bay leaf. Sauté until ham is delicate brown. Add bouillon; bring to boiling point. Add chili powder,

salt, cayenne and rice. Cover and cook slowly 35 to
40 minutes until rice is tender; stir frequently.

You'll want to know: Use canned bouillon in this, or
5 bouillon cubes (beef or chicken) dissolved in 4
cups of water. If using bouillon cubes, omit salt.

PORK CHOPS WITH HOPPIN' JOHN
4 servings

4 pork chops
¼ cup chopped onion
½ cup Uncle Ben's®
   Converted® Rice
1 can (15 to 16 ounces)
   black-eyed peas,
   drained

¾ teaspoon salt
Pepper, cayenne, garlic
   seasoning to taste
2 cups water

Brown pork chops in skillet; if thick, simmer slowly,
covered, to partially cook. Lift out chops and pour
all fat from skillet. Add remaining ingredients and
place chops on top. Bring to a boil. Stir; cover and
lower heat. Cook 20 to 25 minutes or until rice is
tender, most of liquid is absorbed and chops are
done.

Another way: For pork chops with red beans and rice,
substitute a 15-to-16-ounce can of red or kidney
beans, drained, for the black-eyed peas.

Quick Trick: Leftover rice? Warm gently in a little butter. Top
mounds of buttered rice with poached eggs for a breakfast
change. Rice makes a wonderful change-of-pace base for Eggs
Benedict, too.

Quick Trick: Leftover rice? Scramble it with eggs and any leftover
vegetables you have for a good and hearty lunch for the kids. Or,
without the vegetables, for breakfast.

WILD-CHINESE RICE
6 servings

1 box (6 ounces)
Uncle Ben's®
Long Grain &
Wild Rice
1 can (10½ ounces)
condensed cream
of mushroom
soup

1¼ cups water
1 can (16 ounces)
Chinese vege-
tables, drained
6 lean pork chops
Black pepper

Mix contents of box, soup and water in 2-quart casserole. Add Chinese vegetables. Arrange pork chops
on top. Sprinkle with black pepper. Bake 1 hour 20
minutes in 350° F. oven. Serve with Chinese noodles
and soy sauce.

Other ways: Veal chops or chicken may be substituted for the pork chops in this dish.

TENDERLOIN TIPS WITH WILD RICE
4 to 6 servings

1½ to 2 pounds beef
tenderloin strips
6 tablespoons butter
or margarine
1 box (6 ounces)
Uncle Ben's® Long
Grain & Wild Rice

1 can (10¾ ounces)
beef gravy
1¼ cups water
1¾ cups chopped
onion
1⅓ cups green pepper

Cut beef into very thin 2- to 3-inch strips. Brown in
3 tablespoons butter. Add contents of both packets
of Long Grain & Wild Rice, beef gravy and water.
Bring to boil. Cover and cook over low heat until
water is absorbed, about 25 minutes. Meanwhile
sauté onion and green pepper in 3 tablespoons butter
for 3 minutes. Do not overcook. Add to cooked rice
and beef.

COSSACK STEAK, HASH-BROWN RICE

4 servings

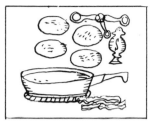

1. Fry 2 slices bacon in a skillet. Drain and crumble; reserve. Season 1¼ pounds ground beef with ¼ teaspoon salt. Make 4 patties.

4. Dissolve 3 beef bouillon cubes in 2 cups boiling water. Add 1 teaspoon Worcestershire sauce, 1 teaspoon ketchup, a dash of pepper.

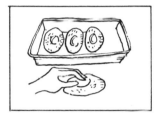

2. Make a well in the top of each patty. Place patties in a metal baking pan. Brown undersides over direct heat. Brown tops of the patties under broiler.

5. Pour bouillon mixture over onion rice. Bring to a boil. Stir, cover and lower heat. Cook until rice is tender and liquid absorbed, about 25 minutes.

3. While patties are browning, make Hash-Brown Rice. Sauté 3 tablespoons chopped onion and ⅔ cup Uncle Ben's® Converted® Rice in 2 tablespoons butter.

6. Fill wells in beef patties with sour cream. Sprinkle with crumbled bacon and 1 tablespoon chopped chives. Place patties on warm platter; surround with rice.

23

GOURMET RICE BEEF STEW 4 to 5 servings

1½ pounds lean
   stewing beef
¼ cup flour
1 teaspoon paprika
1 teaspoon salt
⅛ teaspoon
   powdered
   rosemary
¼ cup cooking oil
1 cup chopped onion
1 clove garlic,
   crushed

½ cup chicken broth
¼ cup dry white wine
   (optional)
½ cup sour cream
3 cups Uncle Ben's®
   Quick Rice
2½ cups water
1½ tablespoons butter
   or margarine
¾ teaspoon salt

Dredge beef in mixture of flour, paprika, salt and rosemary. Reserve remaining flour. Brown beef in hot oil. Drain off excess fat. Add onion and garlic and sauté until soft. Add broth and wine; cover. Simmer until meat is tender, about 1½ hours. Meanwhile combine rice with the water, butter and salt in a saucepan; bring to a vigorous boil; simmer, covered, 5 minutes. Keep hot. When meat is tender, thicken gravy with reserved flour mixture. Stir in sour cream. Heat through. Serve over cooked rice.

FLANK STEAK MEXICANA 5 servings

2½ pounds flank steak
Seasoned meat
   tenderizer
2 slices bacon,
   cooked,
   crumbled
1 tablespoon
   prepared
   horseradish

1 tablespoon
   prepared mustard
2¾ cups water
1 package dry onion
   soup mix
2½ cups Uncle Ben's®
   Quick Rice
1½ tablespoons butter
   or margarine

Sprinkle tenderizer on both sides of meat; puncture with fork. Cut a gash lengthwise in steak to make a pocket. Combine bacon, horseradish and mustard.

Spread in pocket. Secure with half toothpicks. Broil 2 inches from heat 5 to 7 minutes on each side. Stir water and onion soup together in a skillet. Bring to a boil; cook over moderate heat 5 minutes. Stir in rice and butter. Bring to a vigorous boil. Cook over moderate heat, uncovered, about 5 minutes. Cut the broiled steak into very thin slices diagonally across the grain. Serve hot with hot rice.

COUNTRY KITCHEN BRAISED BEEF 4 servings

1¼ pounds beef round, cut 1-inch thick	1 cup sliced onion
¼ cup flour	1 cup sliced carrots
¼ cup fat or oil	¼ teaspoon pepper
1½ cups hot water	1 teaspoon ground marjoram
1 tablespoon Worcestershire sauce	1 cup cooked peas
2 teaspoons salt	1 cup uncooked Uncle Ben's® Converted® Rice

Cut meat into 8 pieces and dredge in flour. Brown slowly in hot fat or oil in heavy skillet. Add any remaining flour and brown. Stir in hot water, Worcestershire sauce and salt. Add onions, and cover. Cook over low heat for 1¼ hours. Add carrots, pepper and marjoram. Continue cooking over low heat for 30 to 45 minutes until meat and carrots are fork tender. Meanwhile cook rice according to package directions. To serve, arrange peas over meat and gravy. Accompany with rice.

To make a meal: Serve hot biscuits, sweet-and-sour green beans with pimiento, squares of lemon cake with fudge frosting.

Quick Trick: Leftover rice? Fold in half as much applesauce, sprinkle with cinnamon or nutmeg and serve it for breakfast or for lunch.

25

BEEF RAGOUT

6 to 8 servings

1. Brown 2 pounds ground beef in a large skillet. Stir in 1 cup water, 1 cup dry red wine, 1 package (1½ ounces) beef stew seasoning mix and mix well.

4. Add 1½ tablespoons butter or margarine to skillet. Bring to a vigorous boil. Cook over moderate heat, covered, until tender, about 5 minutes.

2. Add 1 can (1 pound, 12 ounces) tomatoes. Bring to a boil; turn down heat to moderate and simmer 10 minutes. Stir in 1 jar (1 pound) whole white onions, drained.

5. Stir 1 can (4 ounces) sliced mushrooms, drained, into rice. Turn out the beef ragout with sauce onto a heated platter. Surround the ragout with rice.

3. Add 1 package (9 ounces) frozen cut green beans. Simmer 15 minutes. Combine 3 cups Uncle Ben's® Quick Rice, 3 cups water, ¾ teaspoon salt in a skillet.

6. If you have a small family, serve half as above; mix remaining rice and ragout and freeze. Reheat, covered, in 450° F. oven 30 minutes.

TEXAS JAMBALAYA

4 to 5 servings

1 cup Uncle Ben's®
   Converted® Rice
2 tablespoons
   drippings
¾ cup sliced onion
½ cup diced green
   pepper
1 clove garlic, minced

1 pound lean ground
   beef
2 cans (10½ ounces
   each) condensed
   tomato soup
½ soup can water
2 teaspoons salt
¼ teaspoon pepper

Add uncooked rice to drippings in heavy pan. Stir constantly over medium heat until rice is browned. Add onion, green pepper, garlic and ground beef. Cook, stirring frequently, until meat is browned. Add remaining ingredients. Cover tightly and cook over low heat for approximately 40 minutes until rice and meat are tender and liquid absorbed. (If needed, add more water during the cooking.)

QUICK-DELICIOUS BEEF STROGANOFF

4 to 5 servings

1 pound ground beef
   chuck
½ cup chopped onion
1 clove, garlic
   crushed
1 4-ounce can sliced
   mushrooms,
   drained
1 teaspoon salt
¼ teaspoon pepper
2 tablespoons butter
   or margarine

¼ cup sherry
   (optional)
1 tablespoon lemon
   juice
2 beef bouillon cubes
1½ cups water
2 cups Uncle Ben's®
   Quick Rice
1 cup sour cream
½ teaspoon paprika
1 tablespoon
   chopped parsley

Brown beef, onion, garlic, mushrooms, salt and pepper in butter or margarine. Add sherry, lemon juice, bouillon cubes and water. Cover; simmer 10 minutes. Add rice. Cover; simmer until rice is tender and liquid is absorbed, about 5 minutes. Stir in sour cream. Heat through. Sprinkle with paprika and parsley.

27

MONDAY BEEF BAKE

6 to 8 servings

1½ pounds ground
  beef
1 cup chopped
  onions
1 clove garlic,
  minced
1 tablespoon oil
2 cups sliced celery
1 can (10½ ounces)
  condensed
  mushroom soup

1 package (10 ounces)
  frozen mixed
  vegetables, thawed
2 cups cooked Uncle
  Ben's® Quick Rice
2 tablespoons soy
  sauce
2 teaspoons salt
½ teaspoon pepper
1 can (3 ounces)
  Chinese noodles

Brown meat, onions, and garlic in oil. Add celery and soup and thawed vegetables. Stir in rice and seasonings. Turn into a greased 2½-quart casserole. Cover and bake 25 minutes at 350°. Remove cover and top with noodles. Return to the oven for 5 minutes.

Other ways: Ground lamb (often found at the market in the form of lamb patties) gives a different flavor to this dish. If you have a little leftover vegetable of any sort, by all means add it. And to vary the flavor another way, substitute cream of celery, cream of asparagus or Cheddar cheese soup for the mushroom soup.

To make a meal: Start a busy-day dinner with a citrus-fruit cup (from a jar bought in the market's dairy case, if you like). With the Beef Bake serve lettuce wedges with Russian dressing, toasted, buttered rye bread sprinkled lightly with basil, mixed pickles (from a jar). Finish the meal with vanilla ice cream topped with bottled caramel sauce and sprinkled with chopped walnuts.

STUFFED BEEF ROLLS

4 to 6 servings

2 cups Uncle Ben's®
Quick Rice
1½ pounds round steak,
thinly sliced
½ pound fresh
mushrooms
4 tablespoons butter
or margarine
¼ cup chopped
parsley

¼ cup chopped onion
¼ cup flour
Salt, pepper
3 teaspoons fat
1 can (10½ ounces)
consommé
½ teaspoon dry
mustard

Cook rice according to package directions. Cut steak into 6 equal portions and pound flat. Chop mushroom stems. Melt half the butter; cook stems, parsley and onion 5 minutes. Combine with rice, season to taste. Add remaining butter to pan; cook mushroom caps 5 minutes; reserve. Put generous spoonful of rice mixture on each piece of steak, roll like a jelly roll, secure with string or picks. Mix flour, salt and pepper; dredge beef rolls. Melt fat, brown rolls quickly. Add consommé and mustard, cover, cook slowly about 1 hour or until meat is tender. Reheat rice, covered, over low heat or in a moderate oven. Spoon around beef rolls. Garnish with mushroom caps.

To make a meal: For a company dinner, start with hot tomato bouillon—a dot of sour cream in each serving is a delicious dress-up. French-style green beans, a tossed salad with artichoke hearts and hot apple pie for dessert, topped with slices of Cheddar cheese, round out this meal.

Quick Trick: Leftover rice? Serve it to the children for lunchtime dessert. Mound rice in a sauce dish, pour cream over, give them cinnamon sugar or brown sugar to sprinkle on. Makes a good breakfast dish, too.

TEXAS HASH

6 servings

3 tablespoons fat
½ cup chopped onion
1½ cups chopped
  green pepper
1 pound ground beef
½ cup Uncle Ben's®
  Converted® Rice

2 cups cooked
  tomatoes
1 teaspoon chili
  powder
1 teaspoon salt
¼ teaspoon pepper

Melt fat in a skillet, add onion, green pepper and ground beef; brown well. Add remaining ingredients. Cover tightly. Cook over high heat until steaming freely, then turn heat down and simmer for about 30 minutes.

BEEF PAPRIKASH

4 to 6 servings

1½ pounds beef
3 tablespoons flour
Salt, pepper
3 tablespoons fat
1 onion, diced
1 tablespoon paprika
1 can (10 ounces)
  solid pack
  tomatoes

1 can (6¾ ounces)
  mushrooms
1 cup sour cream
2 cups Uncle Ben's®
  Quick Rice
1⅔ cups water
2 bouillon cubes
1 tablespoon
  chopped parsley

Have beef cut into 1½-inch cubes, dredge in seasoned flour. Melt fat in skillet, brown beef cubes on all sides. Add onion, brown lightly. Add paprika, remaining seasoned flour; stir until smooth. Add liquid from tomatoes (reserve tomatoes). Cook, stirring, until smooth. Add mushrooms with liquid. Cover, simmer 1 hour or until meat is tender. Before serving, stir in sour cream and heat without boiling. Season to taste. Combine rice, water and bouillon cubes. Bring to boil, cover, simmer 5 minutes. Dice and add tomatoes and parsley; toss. Shape bed of rice on serving platter, spoon Beef Paprikash over.

Above, Texas Hash; below, Beef Paprikash

CREOLE OVEN-FRIED CHICKEN AND RICE

6 servings

¼ cup (½ stick) butter
or margarine
1 fryer chicken (2½ to
3 pounds),
disjointed
Flour seasoned with
salt, pepper,
paprika and
poultry seasoning
1 cup Uncle Ben's®
Converted® Rice
½ cup chopped onion

1 cup chopped celery
⅓ cup chopped green
pepper
1 clove garlic,
chopped
2 tablespoons
chopped parsley
1 cup chicken broth
2 cups canned
tomatoes
Salt, pepper, cayenne

Preheat oven to 400° F. Melt butter in a 12- x 9- x 2-inch baking pan. Dredge chicken in seasoned flour. Place in pan, skin side down. Bake, uncovered, 25 to 30 minutes or until lightly browned. Remove from pan. Mix rice with chopped vegetables; distribute mixture over bottom of pan. Return chicken to pan, skin side up. Bring broth, tomatoes and seasonings to the boiling point. Pour over contents of pan, submerging the rice mixture completely. Bake, uncovered, 40 to 45 minutes or until rice and chicken are tender. (Add more liquid during cooking if necessary, to prevent dryness.)

CHICKEN-RICE GOURMET

4 servings

4 chicken breasts
(about 1½
pounds)
2 cups water
½ cup chopped celery
with leaves

1 small bay leaf
1 small onion, sliced
½ teaspoon salt
1 teaspoon grated
orange rind

½ green pepper, cut
in fine strips
1 teaspoon soft
butter or
margarine
1½ tablespoons
cornstarch

1 package (6 ounces)
Uncle Ben's®
Long Grain &
Wild Rice
½ cup dry white wine
(optional)
2 tablespoons orange
juice

Place chicken in saucepan with water, celery, bay leaf, onion and salt. Cover pan and simmer gently for about 1 hour, or until chicken is tender. Meanwhile cook rice as directed on package. Keep hot. When chicken has finished cooking, remove from broth. Strain broth and boil liquid down to make about 1 cup. Add orange rind and green pepper; simmer 5 minutes. Brush chicken with butter or margarine and place under broiler to brown. Combine cornstarch, wine and orange juice. (If wine is eliminated, use all of juice from orange. Add water to make ½ cup.) Add to broth and cook until thickened. Serve on rice. Spoon sauce over the top.

CHICKEN CHOP SUEY   6 servings

2 cups cooked
chicken,
julienned or
diced
3 tablespoons butter
or chicken fat
¾ cup diced green
pepper
1½ cups diced celery
1 cup sliced onions
2 cups canned bean
sprouts, drained
1¼ cups chicken broth
4 tablespoons soy
sauce

1 teaspoon salt
⅛ teaspoon pepper
2 tablespoons
cornstarch
1 cup toasted
almonds
1 can (4 ounces)
mushrooms,
drained
6 cups hot, cooked
Uncle Ben's®
Converted® Rice

33

Brown chicken in butter or chicken fat. Add green pepper, celery and onions; cover and cook over low heat until vegetables are tender, about 20 minutes. Add bean sprouts, chicken broth, soy sauce, salt and pepper; heat to boiling. Blend cornstarch in ¼ cup cold water; add to mixture, stirring, and cook about 10 minutes until thickened. Stir in almonds, mushrooms. Serve with hot rice.

CHICKEN BREASTS WITH WILD RICE
4 to 6 servings

4 chicken breasts
   (about 2 pounds),
   cut in half
¼ cup flour
1½ teaspoons salt
¼ teaspoon pepper
¼ cup cooking oil
1 box (6 ounces)
   Uncle Ben's®
   Long Grain &
   Wild Rice

1 cup hot water
¼ cup white cooking
   wine (optional)
2¼ cups water
1 tablespoon butter
   or margarine

Dredge chicken with flour mixed with 1 teaspoon salt and the pepper. Brown chicken in hot oil, using ovenproof skillet or casserole. Stir in contents of seasoning packet from rice carton. Add 1 cup hot water and the wine. Cover tightly and bake in 325° F. oven, 1 hour or until chicken is tender. During last 30 minutes of cooking time, mix contents of rice packet with ½ teaspoon salt, 2¼ cups of water and butter or margarine in saucepan. Bring to boil; cover. Simmer until water is absorbed, about 25 minutes. Arrange rice on a serving dish. Place chicken on rice. Pour the sauce over rice and chicken.

CHICKEN LOAF

6 to 8 servings

1. Bring 1¼ cups water to a boil. Add ½ cup Uncle Ben's® Converted® Rice, ½ teaspoon salt. Cover; cook over low heat until all water is absorbed, about 25 minutes.

2. Sauté ¼ cup sliced mushrooms in 2 tablespoons butter or margarine. Remove mushrooms from pan. Stir 3 tablespoons flour into butter.

3. Gradually add ⅔ cup milk; cook, stirring, until sauce bubbles and thickens. Combine sauce with cooked rice. Chop cooked chicken to make 2 cups.

4. Add chicken, ¼ cup chopped pecans and reserved mushrooms to rice-sauce mixture. Beat 1 egg well. Add egg to rice-chicken mixture, blend.

5. Pack mixture into a loaf pan. Bake in 350° F. oven for 30 to 35 minutes or until set and nicely browned. While loaf cooks, make Pimiento Sauce.

6. Melt 2 tablespoons butter or margarine in a saucepan. Add 2 tablespoons flour. Stir until smooth. Gradually add 1 cup chicken stock or bouillon.

7. Cook, stirring, until sauce bubbles and thickens. Add 2 tablespoons cream, dash of salt, ⅛ teaspoon thyme, ⅛ teaspoon paprika. Heat briefly.

8. Add 2 tablespoons chopped pimiento. When loaf is done, let stand 5 minutes, then turn out and slice. Serve Pimiento Sauce over slices.

CHICKEN IN THE WILD

4 servings

6 slices bacon
2 large chicken
    breasts, split
¾ cup flour
¾ teaspoon salt
½ teaspoon thyme
¼ teaspoon white
    pepper
¼ teaspoon turmeric
2 chicken bouillon
    cubes

½ cup chopped green
    pepper
½ cup chopped onion
1 package (6 ounces)
    Uncle Ben's®
    Long Grain & Wild
    Rice
1 cup milk or half-and-
    half cream

In a Dutch oven, fry bacon until crisp; remove and reserve. Season flour with salt, thyme, pepper and turmeric. Dredge chicken breasts in flour and reserve remaining flour. Brown breasts in the bacon fat. Dissolve bouillon cubes in 1 cup hot water. Add to chicken; lower heat and simmer, covered, until chicken is tender, about 20 to 25 minutes. Remove chicken breasts and keep them warm. Cook rice according to package directions. Meanwhile add green pepper and onion to liquid in Dutch oven; simmer, covered, five minutes. In a small bowl, blend 3 tablespoons reserved seasoned flour into cold milk or cream. Add gradually to simmering liquid, stirring until mixture bubbles and thickens. Turn out rice on hot serving platter. Top with chicken breasts. Pour sauce over all. Garnish with crumbled bacon.

ALMOND TURKEY DELIGHT

4 servings

3 cups cooked Uncle
    Ben's® Converted®
    Rice
¼ cup almonds
⅓ cup butter or
    margarine
¼ cup flour

1 can (10½ ounces)
    consommé
⅓ cup water
1 teaspoon salt
1 to 2 cups small slices
    (or diced) cooked
    turkey

Sliver almonds and brown lightly in melted butter or margarine. Remove from pan. Blend flour with remaining fat. Add consommé and water slowly and cook over low heat, stirring constantly, until sauce is thickened. Add salt. Place cooked rice in buttered individual casseroles or larger baking dish. Top with turkey, or nestle turkey in center of rice. Sprinkle with toasted almonds and cover with sauce. Bake in 400° F. oven for approximately 20 minutes or until thoroughly heated and sauce bubbles.

GOLD RUSH CHICKEN
5 servings

5 chicken breasts, whole
2 tablespoons concentrated garlic spread
2 tablespoons butter or margarine
2½ cups chicken broth
1 cup Uncle Ben's® Converted® Rice
¼ teaspoon salt
1 cup grated Parmesan cheese
¼ cup chopped pimientos
2 cans (10¾ ounces each) chicken gravy

Arrange chicken in one layer, skin side up, in buttered baking dish. Combine garlic spread and butter; melt. Brush some of this mixture on chicken. Brown in 400° F. oven for 30 minutes, brushing often with remaining garlic butter. Bring broth to a boil. Stir in rice and salt. Cover tightly and cook over low heat until all water is absorbed, about 25 minutes. Stir in ½ cup cheese and the pimientos. Combine gravy and ½ cup cheese. Pour this sauce over chicken; cover dish tightly with foil. Reduce temperature to 350° and bake 15 to 20 minutes or until done. Turn hot rice out on a platter, place chicken and sauce on top.

Another way: For the butter and garlic spread in this recipe, you may substitute ¼ cup ready-to-use garlic spread.

EASY ARROZ CON POLLO

4 to 5 servings

1 broiler-fryer chicken
(3½ pounds), cut
up
⅔ cup butter or
margarine, melted
Salt, pepper, paprika
2 tablespoons butter
or margarine
1 cup Uncle Ben's®
Converted® Rice
2 cans (10½ ounces
each) chicken
broth
¼ teaspoon each
oregano, salt

¼ cup chopped fresh
parsley
For sauce:
1 can (15 ounces)
tomato sauce
1 can (4 ounces) sliced
mushrooms,
drained
1 tablespoon instant
minced onions
1 bay leaf
½ teaspoon oregano

Arrange chicken in one layer, skin side up, in buttered baking dish. Brush with some melted butter; sprinkle generously with salt, pepper, paprika. Brown in 400° F. oven for 30 minutes, brushing often with melted butter. Cook rice in 2 tablespoons butter; stir frequently for even golden-brown color. Add chicken broth, oregano and salt; bring to boil. Cover tightly and cook over low heat until all water is absorbed, about 25 minutes. During the last 5 minutes, stir in parsley.

For Chicken Sauce: Combine tomato sauce, mushrooms, onions, bay leaf and oregano. Pour over chicken; cover dish tightly with foil. Reduce temperature to 350° F. and bake 15 to 20 minutes, or until done. Serve chicken over hot rice.

BAKED FRYER, WILD RICE DRESSING

4 servings

1 package Uncle
Ben's® Long Grain
& Wild Rice Mix

2¾ cups boiling water

Above, Easy Arroz con Pollo; below, Baked Fryer with Wild Rice Dressing

> 2 to 2¼ pound fryer
> (quartered, light-
> ly seasoned and
> brushed with
> melted butter)
>
> For gravy (if desired):
> 2 tablespoons butter or
> margarine
> 2 tablespoons flour
> 1 cup chicken stock
> (well-seasoned)

Preheat oven to 375° F. Place rice and packet of seasonings into a 1½-quart oblong or 2-quart round casserole. Stir in boiling water. Place chicken quarters, skin side up, over rice. Cover tightly with lid or foil. Bake 1 hour or until chicken is tender. Uncover and run under broiler for final browning. To make gravy, brown butter and flour; remove from heat. Add stock and cook, stirring, until thickened. Season to taste.

Another way: Replace ½ cup water in this recipe with ½ cup sherry for a wonderful flavor surprise.

CHICKEN JAMBALAYA   6 servings

> 2 cups Uncle Ben's®
> Quick Rice
> 1 can condensed beef
> bouillon
> ⅓ cup water
> 2 tablespoons sausage
> drippings or oil
> ¼ cup chopped onion
> ½ cup diced green
> pepper
>
> ½ cup chopped celery
> 1½ cups cut-up cooked
> chicken
> 1½ cups diced cooked
> ham
> 1 cup sliced cooked
> sweet sausage
> Salt, pepper
> 1 jar (4 ounces)
> pimientos

Combine rice, beef bouillon and water in saucepan, bring to vigorous boil, cover, simmer 5 minutes. Heat drippings in skillet. Cook onion, green pepper and celery until golden. Add rice, chicken, ham, sausage and seasonings to taste. (At this point, mixture can be covered and stored in refrigerator, or wrapped and frozen. Warm through over very low heat or in oven.) Serve garnished with pimiento strips.

To make a meal: Serve shrimp cocktails, asparagus vinaigrette, hot rolls—or homemade biscuits, if you're feeling ambitious. Ambrosia tops off the dinner.

TWO-WAY CHICKEN, PIMIENTO RICE
8 servings

3 broiler-fryers, 3 pounds each, cut up	¼ cup butter or margarine
Evaporated milk	¾ cup thinly sliced celery
Cornflake crumbs	2 medium onions, chopped
Salt, pepper	
¼ cup butter or margarine, melted	¼ cup chopped pimiento
½ cup chicken consommé	4 cups Uncle Ben's® Quick Rice
¼ cup white wine	3 cups water

Coat half the seasoned chicken pieces with evaporated milk, dip into cornflake crumbs seasoned with salt and pepper. Arrange, cut side down, on foil-covered baking sheet. Put remaining chicken in a casserole; brush with melted butter, season with salt and pepper. Put both pans in oven, bake at 375° F. 25 minutes. Combine chicken consommé and wine. Pour over chicken in casserole and continue baking all chicken 25 minutes or until tender. Meanwhile, melt butter or margarine in skillet. Add celery, onion, pimiento and rice; sauté briefly. Add water; stir. Bring to a vigorous boil; cover and simmer about five minutes. Serve crisp-crusted chicken to the children, sauced chicken to the adults, and the Pimiento Rice to all.

TURKEY POMPOMS

10 servings

1. Dice sufficient leftover turkey, white and dark meat, to make 1⅓ cups. Have ready 3¼ cups cooked Uncle Ben's® Converted® Rice, cooled. Combine with turkey.

4. Add sauce to rice mixture. Stir in ¼ teaspoon poultry seasoning (or an equal amount of mixed sage and thyme), ⅔ teaspoon monosodium glutamate.

2. Add ⅔ cup chopped celery, 3 tablespoons chopped onion, 1½ tablespoons chopped pimiento, 1½ tablespoons chopped parsley, ⅓ cup chopped walnuts.

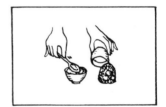

5. Chill mixture for 1 hour or more. Form pompoms by packing mixture into a custard cup, rounding each slightly on top. Turn out and form remainder.

3. Make a medium white sauce by melting 3 tablespoons butter or margarine, adding 3 tablespoons flour; gradually add 1⅔ cups milk. Cook until thickened.

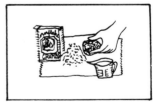

6. Measure 1 cup cornflake crumbs. Roll each pompom gently in crumbs. Place pompoms close together on ungreased pan. Bake in 350° F. oven for 50 minutes.

42

TURKEY WITH HOT WINE SAUCE 6 servings

1. Bring 2½ cups water to a boil. Add 1 cup Uncle Ben's® Converted® Rice and 1 teaspoon salt. Cover tightly and cook over low heat until all water is absorbed, about 25 minutes.

5. Cook, stirring constantly, until thickened. Add 2½ cups grated Swiss cheese and ½ teaspoon salt. Continue to cook, stirring over hot water, until sauce is well thickened and cheese is melted.

2. Meanwhile cut cooked turkey into 6 servings—slices of all white meat or part white meat, part dark per serving.

6. Stir 3 tablespoons port wine into sauce. Cover sauce and keep warm. Dish out rice, dividing equally among 6 serving plates.

3. Cook 24 asparagus spears, fresh or frozen, or put on to heat an equal number of canned asparagus spears.

7. Top each serving with 4 asparagus spears. Place a serving of turkey over each serving of asparagus. Divide hot wine sauce over the servings.

4. Melt ½ cup of butter or margarine in the top of a double boiler, over direct heat. Blend in ½ cup flour. Gradually add 1¾ cups light cream, stirring.

8. *Other ways:* If you like, serve slices of broiled Canadian bacon, placed under the turkey, for a more substantial dish. Or use 2 slices of crisp bacon for each serving.

FEATURE ATTRACTION: FISH

Shellfish, too, in just-right recipes

SHRIMP CREOLE WITH RICE
6 servings

2 tablespoons oil or
  fat
1 cup diced onions
1 cup diced celery
1 clove garlic,
  minced
1 tablespoon flour
1½ teaspoons salt
1 teaspoon chili
  powder (more, if
  desired)

1 cup water
1 teaspoon sugar
2 cups cooked
  tomatoes
1½ cups cooked
  shrimp, deveined
3 cups hot cooked
  Uncle Ben's®
  Converted® Rice

Cook onions, celery and garlic in fat, over low heat, for 10 minutes. Add flour, salt, chili powder that has been blended in a little water, remaining water, sugar and tomatoes, and simmer over low heat 15 minutes. Add shrimp and cook 10 minutes longer. Serve with hot rice.

You'll want to know: As in this recipe, you'll find that a dish which calls for tomatoes usually profits from the addition of a little sugar.

TUNA-IN-A-SKILLET
4 to 6 servings

1 tablespoon oil from
  tuna (or other fat)
1 small onion, sliced
2½ cups canned
  tomatoes

1 bay leaf
Salt, pepper
1 cup Uncle Ben's®
  Converted® Rice
1 can (6½ ounces) tuna

Cook onion in oil in skillet until tender. Stir in tomatoes, seasonings, uncooked rice. Add tuna and cover tightly. Cook over low heat for about 25 minutes until rice is tender and liquid absorbed. (Use more water during cooking if needed.)

44

BAKED FISH FILLETS, RICE DRESSING

4 to 6 servings

1. Cook ¾ cup Uncle Ben's® Converted® Rice according to package directions. Meanwhile sauté 1½ cups chopped celery, ½ cup of chopped onion in 2 tablespoons butter or margarine.

2. Combine celery and onion with cooked rice. Add 1 teaspoon salt, 1 teaspoon poultry seasoning. Place rice mixture in a buttered baking dish.

3. Cut fish fillets in serving pieces. (Use flounder, perch—any fish you like; thaw first if fish is frozen.) Sprinkle the pieces of fillet with salt.

4. Arrange fish over rice. Combine ¼ cup lemon juice with the grated rind of 1 lemon and 3 tablespoons melted butter or margarine. Pour over fish.

5. Bake in a 400° F. oven about 35 minutes until fish flakes easily with a fork. Before bringing to the table, sprinkle with minced parsley.

6. *Other ways:* Grated Parmesan or other sharp cheese, or chopped olives, may be added to the dressing for extra flavor.

45

PAELLA

6 to 7 servings

2 lobsters (1¼ pounds each)
½ cup olive oil
Salt, pepper
1 cup dry white wine
6 large shrimp
12 littleneck clams
12 mussels
½ pound lean pork cut in ½-inch cubes
6 boned chicken breasts (5 to 6 ounces each)
2 red onions, diced
3 red peppers, diced
4 beefsteak tomatoes, coarsely chopped or 1 can (1 pound) tomatoes
1 cup Uncle Ben's® Converted® Rice
⅛ teaspoon saffron
⅛ teaspoon paprika
2½ cups chicken stock or bouillon
5 Spanish sausages (chorizos) sliced ¼-inch thick
½ cup cooked peas

Remove tail and claws from lobsters. Cut tails into 4 pieces and claws into 3. Sauté over medium heat in 4 tablespoons olive oil with dash salt and pepper for about 3 minutes. Add 2 tablespoons wine; set aside.

Devein shrimp and set aside. In deep kettle, boil clams and mussels in lightly salted water just until shells are opened. Remove and clean, cutting out muscle. Set aside. Roast pork cubes without any liquid 20 minutes in a 375° F. oven, stirring often to prevent sticking. Set aside. In large flameproof casserole pan, sauté chicken breasts in 2 tablespoons olive oil just until golden brown. Remove chicken from pan; set aside. Add onions, red peppers and tomatoes to pan juices and cook over medium heat just until onions are transparent but not browned.

Add remainder of olive oil. Add rice and sauté just until golden brown. Add saffron, paprika, stock or bouillon, remainder of wine and salt and pepper to taste. Bring to boil. Arrange lobster pieces and shrimp around edge of pan and chicken breasts in the center.

Right, Paella

Cook 15 minutes in 375° F. oven. Add clams, mussels, pork and chorizos. Cook additional 10 minutes, or until liquid is absorbed and rice is tender. Sprinkle heated cooked peas over all.

QUICK SALMON BECHAMEL
4 servings

1 can (10½ ounces) condensed cream of mushroom soup
½ cup liquid from salmon (part water or milk, if necessary)

Dash nutmeg
1 can (1 pound) salmon
4 cups hot cooked Uncle Ben's® Converted® Rice

Blend cream of mushroom soup, liquid and nutmeg. Heat thoroughly. Break salmon into chunks, remove bones and stir into a sauce. Heat and serve over hot, fluffy rice.

DEVILED SHRIMP ON RICE
4 servings

1½ pounds cooked shrimp, fresh or frozen, shelled and deveined
¼ cup lemon juice
2 tablespoons Worcestershire sauce
½ cup minced onion
¼ cup butter or margarine
¼ cup flour
2 cups milk

1 teaspoon each: curry powder, dry mustard, paprika
1½ teaspoons salt
Dash each: pepper, nutmeg
2 egg yolks, well beaten
4 cups hot cooked Uncle Ben's® Converted® Rice

Reserve several whole shrimp for garnish. Dice remaining shrimp and marinate in lemon juice and Worcestershire sauce several hours. Cook onion, until tender, in melted butter or margarine. Remove from heat and blend in flour. Add milk gradually.

Cook over low heat, stirring constantly, until sauce is thickened. Drain shrimp and combine remaining seasonings with lemon juice and Worcestershire sauce. Beat egg yolks with seasonings and stir into sauce. Add diced shrimp and heat thoroughly. Serve over hot, fluffy rice. Garnish with whole shrimp—dip tails in paprika for extra color.

EAST INDIAN SHRIMP CURRY   4 servings

1 cup Uncle Ben's®
   Converted® Rice
2 medium onions,
   chopped
1 clove garlic,
   chopped
¼ cup butter or
   margarine

4 teaspoons curry
   powder
1 can (6 ounces)
   tomato paste
4 tablespoons flour
¼ cup cold water
2 pounds fresh shrimp

Cook rice according to package directions. Press rice into oiled ring mold. Brown onions and garlic lightly in butter or margarine. Add curry powder, lightly brown. Add tomato paste. Mix flour to smooth paste in cold water; add. Wash shrimp in cold running water; put into boiling salted water. Cover; boil 15 to 20 minutes. Drain, reserving 2½ cups liquid. Add to tomato mixture; bring to boiling point. Cook, stirring constantly, about 10 minutes. Shell shrimp, add to sauce; heat. Unmold rice on serving dish, fill center with shrimp mixture.

You'll want to know: Curry is always improved by serving condiments with it, as people do in India. Serve as many of the following as suits your taste: grated coconut, chopped peanuts, chutney (buy it bottled, sweet or sour, or both), plumped raisins, diced cucumber, chopped hard-cooked eggs. Let each diner sprinkle these condiments, singly or in combination, over his serving of Shrimp Curry.

Above, Seafood Creole; below, Fish and Rice Bake

SEAFOOD CREOLE

4 servings

½ cup chopped onion
¾ cup chopped celery
¼ cup chopped green
    pepper
1 clove garlic, minced
2 tablespoons cooking
    oil
2 cups Uncle Ben's®
    Quick Rice
1 pound raw shrimp
    (shelled)

1 cup water
1 can (8 ounces)
    stewed tomatoes
1 beef bouillon cube
Salt, pepper
1 bay leaf
⅛ teaspoon thyme
1 can (7½ ounces)
    crab meat, drained

In a large skillet, sauté onion, celery, green pepper and garlic in oil until golden. Add rice, shrimp and remaining ingredients except crab meat Bring to vigorous boil, stir and cover. Cook over low heat 15 minutes. Add crab meat; heat.

FISH AND RICE BAKE

8 servings

1 cup Uncle Ben's®
    Converted® Rice
2¼ cups water
1½ teaspoons salt
3 tablespoons butter
    or margarine
1 small onion,
    chopped
4 large stalks celery,
    chopped
3 tablespoons finely
    chopped ripe
    olives
1 tablespoon
    Worcestershire
    sauce

½ teaspoon sage
1 teaspoon dried
    parsley flakes
¼ teaspoon cayenne
    or red pepper
2 pounds fish fillets,
    fresh or frozen
    (cut in 8 portions)
Butter or margarine
Salt, lemon juice,
    paprika
Lemon slices

Melt butter or margarine in a large saucepan; add onions and celery. Cover and cook over low heat, 10 minutes. Add water, rice and salt. Bring to a boil; cover. Reduce heat and cook until water is absorbed and rice is just tender, about 20 minutes. Add olives, Worcestershire sauce, sage, parsley flakes and cayenne. Spread into a glass baking dish. Top with fish fillets; dot with butter or margarine, sprinkle with salt, lemon juice and paprika. Bake in 325° F. oven, about 45 minutes or until fish is tender. Garnish with lemon slices.

LOUISIANA SHRIMP
6 to 8 servings

2 cups Uncle Ben's® Converted® Rice
6 tablespoons fat or bacon drippings
4 tablespoons flour
1 cup chopped celery
2 cups chopped onion
1 cup chopped green pepper
4 cloves garlic, minced
2 pounds shrimp
2 teaspoons salt
2 teaspoons black pepper (red pepper, if desired)
1 bay leaf
2 tablespoons chopped parsley

Cook rice according to directions on the package. Meanwhile, heat fat in heavy skillet; add flour. Brown thoroughly, stirring constantly. Add other vegetables and cook until soft, about 25 minutes. Place cleaned shrimp and 2 quarts water in 1-gallon saucepan. Add all seasonings except parsley and then add flour-vegetable mixture. Simmer for 1 hour. Add parsley in last 10 minutes of cooking time. Serve over rice.

Quick Trick: Leftover rice? Use it as the base for creamed eggs or Eggs Goldenrod—a nice change from the usual toast.

GREAT GO-ALONGS

Tasty rice-based side dishes

ITALIAN BAKED RICE

4 servings

3 cups cooked
  Uncle Ben's®
  Converted® Rice
¼ cup chopped
  pimiento
¼ cup chopped green
  pepper
⅓ cup chopped onion
¼ teaspoon paprika
1 teaspoon
  Worcestershire
  sauce

1 cup grated
  sharp cheese
1 teaspoon salt
1½ cups cooked or
  canned tomatoes
1 tablespoon butter
  or margarine

Combine rice, pimiento, green pepper, onion, paprika, Worcestershire sauce and half of cheese. Blend well. Turn into buttered 1½-quart baking dish and sprinkle with remaining cheese. Add salt to tomatoes and place on rice. Dot with butter or margarine and bake in a 350° F. oven for approximately 30 minutes.

SKILLET FRIED RICE

4 to 6 servings

2 tablespoons butter
  or margarine
1 cup Uncle Ben's®
  Converted® Rice
1 can (2 ounces)
  sliced
  mushrooms

½ small onion, thinly
  sliced
1¼ cups consommé or
  bouillon
1 cup water
1 teaspoon salt
¼ teaspoon pepper

Melt butter or margarine in skillet over medium heat. Add uncooked rice and brown lightly, stirring occasionally. Drain mushrooms; reserve liquid. Add mushrooms and sliced onion to skillet. Continue cooking until rice is well browned and onion is tender. Add consommé, water, liquid from mushrooms and seasonings. Bring to boil. Reduce heat and cover skillet. Cook over low heat until rice is tender and liquid absorbed, 20 to 25 minutes.

53

RICE A LA GRECQUE

6 servings

This goes especially well with curried
main dishes based on either meat or poultry

1 cup chopped
    onions
2 tablespoons butter
    or margarine
2½ cups Uncle Ben's®
    Quick Rice

2 cups chicken broth
⅔ cup green peas
⅔ cup golden raisins
¼ teaspoon salt
⅓ cup grated
    Parmesan cheese

Cook onions in melted butter in medium skillet until soft. Stir in rice, broth, peas, raisins and salt. Bring to a vigorous boil. Cook over moderate heat, uncovered, about 5 minutes. Stir in grated cheese. Serve hot.

ONION RICE CUSTARD

6 servings

Here's a quiche-like custard with
the goodness of rice to give it body

3 onions, thinly
    sliced and
    separated into
    rings
2 tablespoons butter
    or margarine
1 cup Uncle Ben's®
    Quick Rice

1 cup milk
1½ teaspoons salt
¼ teaspoon black
    pepper
6 eggs, beaten

Sauté onions in butter or margarine until clear (do not brown). Bring rice, milk, salt and pepper to a boil. Let cook 3 minutes. Stir in onions and eggs. Pour into 1½-quart casserole. Bake for 30 to 40 minutes in a 350° F. oven.

To make a meal: Serve with broiled ham slices, buttered green beans, pineapple upside-down cake.

Quick Trick: Leftover rice? Heat gently in leftover (or canned, or from-a-mix) gravy for lunch—particularly good if the leftover rice happens to be Uncle Ben's® Long Grain & Wild.

54

Right, Rice à la Grecque

PATIO TOMATOES

6 servings

6 large tomatoes
1 cup Uncle Ben's®
    Converted® Rice
1½ cups grated cheese
6 slices chopped
    crisp bacon
¾ cup chopped onion

½ teaspoon salt
Dash pepper
¼ teaspoon ground
    thyme (optional)
2 tablespoons
    minced parsley or
    celery tops

Cut stem ends off tomatoes. Scoop out pulp and save for soup or sauce. Salt inside of tomatoes and invert to drain. Cook rice by directions on package, and cool. Sauté onion in bacon drippings until tender. Combine bacon, onion, cheese and seasonings with cooked rice. Pack mixture in tomatoes and place in centers of 12-inch foil squares, heavy duty or 2 thicknesses regular. (If tomatoes do not hold all of rice mixture, make a separate foil packet for the hungriest in the crowd.) Gather foil ends and twist slightly. Place on hot grill, allowing about 25 minutes for tomatoes to soften and rice to heat thoroughly. To serve, roll foil back, forming cups for tomatoes.

RICE-CORN PUDDING

6 servings

1½ cups Uncle Ben's®
    Quick Rice
1⅓ cups water
1 tablespoon butter
    or margarine
⅓ teaspoon salt
2 cups cream-style
    canned corn
3 eggs, separated
¼ teaspoon black
    pepper

1½ teaspoons salt
3 tablespoons
    minced onion
¼ teaspoon baking
    powder
1 slice bacon, cut in
    1-inch pieces
1 ounce process
    American cheese,
    cut in squares

Combine rice, water, butter or margarine, and salt; cook as directed on the package. Combine cooked

Above, Patio Tomatoes; below, Rice-Corn Pudding

rice with corn in a 2-quart casserole. Blend in slightly beaten egg yolks, pepper, salt, onion and baking powder. Beat egg whites until stiff; fold in rice mixture. Top with bacon and cheese. Bake in a 350° F. oven 25 to 35 minutes or until top is firm.

RICE 'N' GIBLETS

½ pound chicken
giblets, minced
1 clove garlic,
crushed
2 tablespoons bacon
drippings
1 package Uncle
Ben's® Long
Grain & Wild
Rice

2½ cups water
2 tablespoons
chopped green
onion tops
2 teaspoons chopped
parsley
Dash red pepper

Sauté giblets and garlic in bacon drippings. Add entire contents of rice package and water, and follow directions for cooking on rice box. When done, fold in green onion, parsley and red pepper.

MEXICAN BAKED RICE   6 servings

4 cups cooked
Uncle Ben's®
Converted® Rice
½ cup chopped
pimiento
½ cup finely diced
onion
¼ cup diced green
pepper
2 teaspoons salt

¼ teaspoon pepper
Dash of cayenne
1 teaspoon
Worcestershire
sauce
¾ cup grated cheese
2½ cups canned or
cooked tomatoes
2 tablespoons butter
or margarine

Combine rice, pimiento, onion, green pepper, seasonings, Worcestershire sauce and half of the grated cheese. Stir to blend. Turn into well-buttered 2-quart casserole. Add tomato pulp and juice. Top with remaining cheese and dot with butter. Bake in a 350° F. oven for 30 minutes.

RICE VALENCIA
4 to 6 servings

1 cup Uncle Ben's®
   Converted® Rice
2 tablespoons
   chicken fat,
   butter or
   margarine
¼ cup minced onion
¼ cup minced green
   pepper
1 clove garlic,
   crushed

1 teaspoon paprika
¼ teaspoon chopped
   capers
Dash oregano
3 stuffed green
   olives, sliced
2½ cups chicken stock
   or bouillon

Sauté rice in melted fat until golden brown. Add remaining ingredients. Bring to boil; cover. Simmer until water is absorbed, about 25 minutes.

RICE WITH CREOLE SAUCE
4 to 6 servings

¼ cup chopped onion
¼ cup chopped green
   pepper
¼ cup chopped celery
1 clove garlic,
   crushed
1 can (4 ounces)
   sliced
   mushrooms,
   drained
7 tablespoons butter
   or margarine

2 tablespoons flour
1 can (10½ ounces)
   tomato puree
1¾ cups beef stock
1 teaspoon sugar
¼ teaspoon salt
Dash black pepper
1 cup Uncle Ben's®
   Converted® Rice

Sauté onion, green pepper, celery, garlic and mushrooms in 3 tablespoons butter for 10 minutes. Meanwhile simmer 4 tablespoons butter with the flour for 5 minutes until dark brown. Add sautéed vegetables, tomato puree, beef stock, sugar, salt and pepper. Simmer 1 hour. Cook rice according to directions on package. Serve the sauce over a bed of cooked rice.

59

CREAMY PILAF

6 servings

Remember this perfect go-with the next
time you plan on serving pork chops

2¼ cups chicken stock
1 tablespoon lemon
juice
1½ teaspoons salt
¼ teaspoon pepper
1 bay leaf
2 tablespoons butter
or margarine

3 cups Uncle Ben's®
Quick Rice
1 can (4 ounces)
sliced mush-
rooms, drained
1 cup sour cream
Chopped chives

Combine chicken stock, lemon juice, salt, pepper, bay leaf, butter and rice in a 3-quart saucepan. Heat to boiling, stir once. Cover and simmer about 5 minutes or until liquid is absorbed. Remove bay leaf. Stir in mushrooms and sour cream. Heat through. Sprinkle with chopped chives just before serving.

ALMOND-ONION RICE

4 servings

Looking for something different to
serve with roast chicken? Here it is!

1 cup chopped green
onions and tops
½ cup slivered
almonds
2 tablespoons butter
or margarine,
melted

1⅔ cups chicken broth
2 cups Uncle Ben's®
Quick Rice
½ teaspoon salt

Cook onions and almonds in butter until golden but not brown. Add broth, rice and salt. Heat to boiling; cover and simmer for 5 minutes or until liquid is absorbed.

Another way: Make this with beef broth to serve with roast beef—another flavor, every bit as good.

SPRING RICE CUSTARD

6 servings

Serve this as an out-of-the-ordinary
side dish with baked or broiled ham

2 packages (10 ounces
  each) frozen
  chopped spinach
2 cups cooked Uncle
  Ben's® Converted®
  Rice
6 eggs, slightly beaten
3 tablespoons melted
  butter or margarine

½ cup grated onion
1¼ teaspoons salt
¼ teaspoon pepper
1 tablespoon vinegar
½ cup grated
  Parmesan cheese
1½ cups milk, scalded

Cook spinach according to package directions; drain
well. Combine with rice, eggs, butter, onion, seasonings, vinegar and cheese. Add hot milk, stirring
thoroughly. Turn into a buttered 2-quart casserole.
Set in a pan of hot water and bake in a 350° F. oven
for 1 hour or until custard is set.

SAFFRON RICE

5 to 6 servings

1 cup Uncle Ben's®
  Converted® Rice
¼ cup chopped onion
2 to 3 tablespoons
  butter or margarine

2½ cups chicken stock
  or broth
¼ teaspoon saffron

Sauté rice and onion in butter until golden. Add
chicken stock and saffron. Stir well. Bring to a boil;
cover, lower heat. Cook gently for about 25 minutes
or until all liquid is absorbed. Season with salt and
pepper if needed.

Other ways: Sprinkled with Parmesan cheese, this
makes a good luncheon dish. For extra taste and
color, stir in 2 tablespoons chopped parsley before
sprinkling with cheese.

61

RICE WITH MUSHROOMS A LA DORO'S
6 servings

2 cups chopped
    onions
¼ cup butter or
    margarine
2 cups sliced
    mushrooms
2½ cups chicken broth
1¼ cups Uncle Ben's®
    Converted® Rice

¼ teaspoon each
    salt, pepper
Pinch saffron
¼ cup minced
    prosciutto ham
⅓ cup grated
    Parmesan cheese

Cook onions in melted butter until golden; add mushrooms and cook about 4 minutes. Add chicken broth and bring to a boil. Stir in rice, salt, pepper and saffron. Cover tightly and cook over low heat for 20 minutes. Stir in prosciutto and continue for 5 minutes longer or until water is absorbed. Stir in cheese. Serve hot.

"SPRING HARVEST" RICE RING
6 to 8 servings

1½ cups Uncle Ben's®
    Converted® Rice,
    uncooked
½ cup chopped onion
¼ cup butter or
    margarine

3½ cups hot water
1½ teaspoons salt
½ pound sliced
    process Cheddar
    cheese
¼ cup bread crumbs

Melt butter or margarine in heavy skillet. Add uncooked rice and onion and stir over low heat until golden brown. Add water and salt. Cook, covered, over low heat until water is absorbed and rice is tender—about 25 minutes. Sprinkle bread crumbs in well-buttered ring mold. Alternate layers of cooked rice and sliced cheese in mold—packing tightly. Bake at 350° F. for 10 minutes. Unmold on hot serving platter and fill with favorite creamed vegetables, or use Harvest Vegetable Sauce (see page 64).

Above, Rice with Mushrooms à la Doro's; below, "Spring Harvest" Rice Ring

Harvest Vegetable Sauce

⅓ cup butter or
   margarine
½ cup flour
2 cups milk
1 teaspoon salt
Dash pepper
Dash marjoram and
   garlic, if desired

2 cups cooked
   vegetables (peas
   and carrots—or
   any other
   combination)

Melt butter or margarine in saucepan. Remove from heat and stir in flour. Add milk slowly, stirring constantly. Continue stirring and cook over low heat until thickened. Add seasonings and vegetables.

Another way: For a heartier dish, add sliced hard-cooked eggs to Harvest Vegetables—or, for "pretty," chop the whites and add to sauce; drift the yolks, grated or sieved, over the top.

GOLDEN PEANUT RICE   6 servings

Rice with a perky flavor that
complements veal or chicken perfectly

½ cup raisins
¼ teaspoon curry
   powder or
   turmeric
3 tablespoons butter
   or margarine,
   melted
⅓ cup finely chopped
   parsley

¼ cup finely chopped
   peanuts
¼ teaspoon salt
4 cups hot cooked
   Uncle Ben's®
   Converted® Rice

Soak raisins in hot water until soft; drain. Blend curry powder into butter. Mix all ingredients into hot rice.

RICE WITH A FOREIGN ACCENT

Dishes from all around the globe

GREEK PILAF
6 servings

2½ cups chicken stock
    or chicken
    bouillon
1 tablespoon lemon
    juice
1½ teaspoon salt
1 bay leaf

¼ teaspoon white
    pepper
¼ to ½ cup butter or
    margarine
1 cup Uncle Ben's®
    Converted® Rice

Heat chicken stock, lemon juice, salt, bay leaf, white pepper and half the butter or margarine in top of double boiler. Add rice. Cover and cook 35 minutes over boiling water, stirring occasionally. Remove from heat; turn into a well-buttered casserole, 1½-quart size; top with remaining butter, cover, bake in a moderate oven, 350° F., 10 minutes. Serve hot.

DUTCH CABBAGE ROLLS
6 servings

1 small head green
    cabbage
2½ cups cooked
    Uncle Ben's®
    Converted® Rice
1 pound ground beef

2 tablespoons finely
    diced onion
1 teaspoon salt
⅛ teaspoon pepper
1 egg, beaten
1½ cups tomato juice

Wash, drain cabbage. Cook in boiling salted water until leaves are tender and pliable. Drain; remove outer leaves, reserving 6 large ones. Combine rice, beef, onion, seasonings and egg, stirring to blend. Shape into 6 rolls and place each in center of cabbage leaf; fold or roll and fasten with toothpicks. Place seam side down in casserole. Add tomato juice. Cover and bake in a moderate 350° F. oven for 1 hour. Serve hot with tomato sauce.

RISOTTO

6 servings

2 tablespoons fat
1 small onion
1 cup Uncle Ben's®
    Converted® Rice

2½ cups meat stock or
    broth
Grated cheese (if
    desired)

Heat the fat and brown the chopped onion and rice in it. Add the stock or broth and cook until the rice is tender and the liquid has been absorbed. Taste, and add salt if necessary. Just before serving, a little grated cheese may be stirred in.

Other ways with Risotto: You think of Italy and you immediately think "pasta"—but rice is also a staple Italian food, and those ingenious cooks have thought up many good risotto variations. Here are some of them (with their Italian names) that you may want to experiment with. Start with the basic rice-cooked-in-stock recipe above, and go as far as you like.

Risotto alla Certosina	Rice with crayfish, mushrooms, peas
Risotto alla Finanziera	Rice with chicken livers
Risotto alla Milanese	Rice with marrow, mushrooms, saffron, butter
Risotto con Funghi	Rice with mushrooms
Risotto con Gamberi	Rice with shrimp
Risotto con Salsa di Pesce	Rice with fish sauce
Risotto con Vongole	Rice with clams
Risotto Florentine	Rice with beef marrow, butter, tomatoes, cheese, truffles
Risotto Paesano	Rice with beans, vegetables
Risotto Piemontese	Rice with white truffles
Risotto Torinese	Rice with mushrooms, ham, peppers, safron, diced tomatoes

PARTY FONDUE

6 servings

1. Bring 1¼ cups chicken broth to a boil. Add ½ cup Uncle Ben's® Converted® Rice. Cover tightly; cook over low heat until all liquid is absorbed, about 25 minutes. Cool.

2. Beat 2 eggs lightly. Combine with cooked rice, ¾ cup crumbled crackers, 1 tablespoon minced onion, 1 tablespoon parsley flakes, 3 tablespoons melted butter or margarine.

3. Mix well. Chill until mixture holds together. Form into 1-inch balls. Place on baking pan; bake in 450° F. oven 15 minutes or until brown (makes 40 balls).

4. While rice balls bake, make fondue. Peel 1 clove garlic and rub over the bottom of a chafing dish. Mix 4 cups (1 pound) grated Swiss cheese with 1½ tablespoons flour.

5. Heat 1½ cups milk (or white wine, if you prefer) in chafing dish until almost to boiling point. Add floured cheese slowly, stirring constantly as cheese melts.

6. Season cheese mixture with 1 teaspoon salt, ⅛ teaspoon white pepper, dash nutmeg. When mixture comes to a boil, serve at once; keep bubbling in chafing dish.

7. Each diner spears a rice ball with a fork, "dunks" in the fondue, twirls to capture dribbles, cools the ball a moment, eats the ball—and repeats.

8. *To make a meal:* For a party, serve cooked ham cubes to dip in fondue as well; crisp vegetable relishes and olives, mixed fruit with minted sour cream for dessert.

67

ENSALADA ESPANOLA

4 to 6 servings

A saffron-flavored Spanish rice
salad with little nuggets of fish

½ teaspoon powdered
    saffron
½ cup dry white wine
2 cups hot chicken
    stock
4 cups Uncle Ben's®
    Converted® Rice
Salt, pepper
8 tablespoons olive oil
3 tablespoons wine
    vinegar

4 tablespoons finely
    chopped parsley
1 clove garlic, finely
    chopped
½ teaspoon dry
    mustard
¾ cooked flaked fish
4 small tomatoes,
    quartered
4 hard-cooked eggs,
    quartered

Dissolve saffron in wine; add to hot chicken stock in saucepan. Bring to boil, add rice. Cover, cook over low heat until liquid is absorbed and rice is tender, about 25 minutes. Season to taste with salt and pepper. While rice is cooking, make a dressing of the olive oil, vinegar, garlic, parsley and mustard. Toss cooked hot rice and fish with dressing and taste for seasoning. Garnish with tomatoes, hard-cooked eggs.

You'll want to know: In Spain this salad is generally served at room temperature. It is most often made with cod, but haddock or flounder will make a fine salad, too.

OEUFS GRAND DUC

4 to 5 servings

One of the many wonderful French ways with
eggs—this with a delicate cheese sauce

1 cup chopped onion
2 tablespoons butter
    or margarine
2¼ cups chicken stock
    or bouillon

1 cup Uncle Ben's®
    Converted® Rice
1 bay leaf
Hard-cooked eggs—2
    per serving

Sauté onion in butter or margarine until golden

brown. Add stock or bouillon and bring to boil. Stir in rice and bay leaf; cover. Simmer until water is absorbed, about 25 minutes. Arrange wedges of eggs over bed of rice. Cover with Mornay Sauce. Place under hot broiler and broil until sauce is golden.

Mornay Sauce
2 tablespoons butter
  or margarine
2 tablespoons flour
¼ teaspoon salt
1 cup milk or light
  cream

2 egg yolks
2 tablespoons grated
  cheese

Melt butter or margarine. Blend in flour and salt. Gradually stir in milk. Cook, stirring constantly, until mixture thickens. Beat in egg yolks and cheese. Heat only until cheese melts.

RISI AL TONNO
6 servings

Quick, easy, and absolutely delicious—
what more could you ask? This one's Italian

1 clove garlic
4 tablespoons olive oil
6 tablespoons tomato
  paste
1 cup water
½ teaspoon ground
  basil
2 cans (7 ounces each)
  tuna fish

6 anchovy fillets
Salt
3 cups hot cooked
  Uncle Ben's®
  Converted® Rice
Chopped parsley
Butter or margarine

Stick garlic clove several times with a fork. Sauté in olive oil until golden; discard garlic. Mix tomato paste, water, basil, and add to oil. Simmer 30 minutes. Separate tuna into bite-size chunks. Finely chop anchovies. Add both to sauce; taste and add salt, if necessary. Simmer 15 minutes, stirring occasionally. Sprinkle rice with parsley and dot with butter. Serve with tuna sauce.

REISBOULETTEN MIT SENFSOSSE   6 servings

German rice croquettes with a good, tangy mustard sauce

1. Bring 1¼ cups water to a boil. Add ½ cup Uncle Ben's® Converted® Rice, ½ teaspoon salt. Cover and simmer until all liquid is absorbed, about 25 minutes.

2. Meanwhile thoroughly drain 1 can (16 ounces) sauerkraut, pressing out as much liquid as possible. Beat 2 eggs slightly. Mince sufficient onion to make ⅓ cup.

3. Put sauerkraut, onion and ½ pound frankfurters through food grinder, using medium blade. Add sauerkraut mixture, rice and 1 cup grated Cheddar cheese to eggs.

4. Season with 1 teaspoon salt, ¼ teaspoon pepper. Mix thoroughly. Chill at least 1 hour. Beat another egg slightly; add 2 tablespoons water.

5. Shape chilled mixture into 12 croquettes. Measure 1 cup fine dry bread crumbs onto waxed paper. Dip croquette in crumbs, then egg, then crumbs again.

6. Heat deep fat for frying to 375° F. Fry croquettes in fat until golden brown, about 3 minutes. (Fry only as many croquettes at one time as pan will easily accommodate.)

7. Keep croquettes hot in a low oven. In top of double boiler combine ¾ cup salad dressing (homemade or commercial) with ½ cup cream, 1 tablespoon lemon juice.

8. Stir in 3 tablespoons prepared mustard. Heat over boiling water until very hot. Serve this mustard sauce over croquettes. Garnish with lemon.

POLYNESIAN PORK **4 servings**

A new and bright and quick idea
for serving leftover roast pork

2 stalks celery, finely
    chopped
1 medium onion,
    finely chopped
1 clove garlic, minced
6 tablespoons butter
    or margarine
1 cup Uncle Ben's®
    Converted® Rice
½ teaspoon salt

⅛ teaspoon pepper
Juice and shredded rind
    of one orange
2 cups chicken stock
2 bananas, cut in
    1-inch slices
1 to 2 cups cold roast
    pork in ½-inch
    cubes

Sauté celery, onion, garlic in 4 tablespoons melted
butter until soft but not brown. Stir in rice, salt and
pepper, orange juice and rind, chicken stock. Bring
to a boil; cover and simmer about 25 minutes or until
liquid is absorbed. Meanwhile melt 2 tablespoons
butter in another pan; sauté bananas until golden,
turning once. Stir pork into rice and turn out into
shallow serving dish. Surround with banana slices
sprinkled, if desired, with additional orange rind.

OSSO BUCO CON RISOTTO **4 to 5 servings**

Italian veal shanks—all the tastier
because the meat is left on the bone

Salt, pepper
4 to 5 8-ounce shanks
    of veal with bone
    (from hind legs)
¼ cup plus 2 table-
    spoons flour
2 tablespoons
    cooking oil

1 cup Marsala wine
1 diced carrot
2 diced celery stalks
1½ plus ¾ cups
    chopped onion
2 diced shallots
1 clove garlic,
    crushed

71

1 can (2 ounces)
sliced
mushrooms
¼ teaspoon salt
2 teaspoons
Kitchen Bouquet
2 tablespoons butter
or margarine

1 cup Uncle Ben's®
Converted® Rice
2½ cups chicken stock
or bouillon
1 cup dry white wine

Salt and pepper meat and roll in ¼ cup flour. Brown in oil. Remove excess fat. Add Marsala, carrot, celery, 1½ cups onion, shallots, garlic, mushrooms (with liquid) and salt. Bring to boil; cover. Simmer for 15 to 20 minutes or until meat is tender. Meanwhile sauté remaining onion in butter or margarine until golden. Stir in rice, remaining ingredients. Bring to boil; cover. Simmer till water is absorbed, about 25 minutes. Remove meat from sauce and strain away vegetables. Add 2 tablespoons flour to sauce and cook until thickened. To serve, place meat on bed of rice and cover with sauce.

VEAL MARSALA WITH RISOTTO   4 servings

1 pound thinly sliced
veal cut for
scaloppine
Flour, salt, pepper
¼ cup butter or
margarine
1 cup thinly sliced
mushrooms
¼ cup hot water
1 beef bouillon cube
¼ cup Marsala or
white wine

Salt, cayenne, pepper
3 tablespoons butter
or margarine
1 medium onion,
thinly sliced
½ red pepper or
pimiento, slivered
2 cups Uncle Ben's®
Quick Rice
1 can condensed beef
bouillon
¼ cup water

Coat veal slices with seasoned flour. Melt butter in large skillet, brown veal on both sides. Add mushrooms, cook until golden. Stir in hot water and bouillon cube, scraping pan. Cook a few minutes until veal is tender. Add wine, heat, add seasonings to taste. Serve in ring of risotto.

Risotto: Melt butter in saucepan. Sauté onion and pepper lightly. Add rice, bouillon and water. Bring to vigorous boil; cover. Simmer 5 minutes.

To make a meal: Serve antipasto, sautéed zucchini, a layered vegetable salad, Biscuit Tortoni for dessert.

Quick Trick: Leftover rice? Cook one package of lemon pie filling mix according to directions. Add 1 cup cold cooked rice; cool. Fold in ½ cup heavy cream, whipped; chill. Sprigs of mint make a pretty and tasty garnish.

PILAF DE FOIE DE VOLAILLE   4 to 6 servings

A French way with rice and chicken
livers that is truly delicious

1 cup chopped onion	Salt, pepper
4 tablespoons butter	1 pound chicken livers
or margarine	2 tablespoons butter
1 cup Uncle Ben's®	or margarine
Converted® Rice	1 can (8 ounces) tomato
1 teaspoon salt	sauce
1 bay leaf	Parsley
2½ cups water	

Sauté onions in 2 tablespoons butter or margarine until golden brown. Add rice and sauté lightly. Add salt, bay leaf and water. Bring to boil; cover. Simmer until water is absorbed, about 25 minutes. Meanwhile, salt and pepper chicken livers and sauté in butter about 8 to 10 minutes. Add tomato sauce and cook 3 to 5 minutes—just until heated through. Serve over bed of cooked rice. Garnish with parsley.

SPANISH PICNIC SALAD
6 servings

2 cups cold cooked
Uncle Ben's®
Converted® Rice
½ cup cold cooked
cubed carrots
½ cup cold cooked
cauliflower
⅓ cup olive oil
1 tablespoon lemon
juice

1 teaspoon onion juice
2 teaspoons wine
vinegar
1 teaspoon celery seed
½ teaspoon dry
mustard
Dash coarse-ground
black pepper
2 tablespoons drained
capers

Combine rice and vegetables. Make a Sauce Vinaigrette by combining oil, lemon juice, onion juice, vinegar, celery seed, dry mustard, salt and pepper. Use enough of this just to hold salad together. Sprinkle capers over top.

Other ways: Many things can be added to extend this salad—tuna fish, sardines, anchovies or diced cold meat or poultry. Use a bit more Sauce Vinaigrette.

SPANISH RICE AND CHICKEN
4 to 5 servings

1 fryer, quartered
¼ cup olive oil
⅓ cup chopped
Spanish onion
½ cup chopped green
pepper
Dash nutmeg
1 clove garlic, crushed
1 can (4 ounces) tomatoes

½ teaspoon
powdered
saffron
1¾ cups water
½ bay leaf
1 teaspoon salt
1 cup Uncle Ben's®
Converted® Rice

Sauté chicken in olive oil for 10 minutes. Drain off excess oil. Add onion, green pepper, nutmeg, garlic and tomatoes. Cook for 15 minutes stirring occasionally. Dissolve saffron in water. Add water, bay leaf and salt. Bring to boil. Arrange rice in bottom of 2½-quart casserole. Arrange browned chicken on top, then pour liquid over all; cover. Bake 30 to 35 minutes at 425° F. or until chicken and rice are tender.

MADRAS CURRY

4 to 6 servings

Here's a truly satisfying curry, magnificently
flavored, with a bonus of sautéed bananas

1 medium onion, thinly sliced	2 to 4 teaspoons curry powder
1/2 green pepper, chopped	1 teaspoon salt
1 small clove garlic, finely chopped	1/8 teaspoon pepper
3 tablespoons olive oil, butter or margarine	1 large bay leaf
	1 pinch thyme
	2 whole cloves
2 tablespoons flour	Dash ground mace
2 cups meat stock or bouillon	2 1/2 to 3 cups cooked lamb, cut in small cubes
1/2 cup tomato sauce	3 bananas, sliced about 1/2 inch thick
2 tablespoons minced parsley	Saffron Rice (below)

Sauté onion, green pepper and garlic in 2 tablespoons
oil or butter until golden brown. Sprinkle the flour
on top. Stir until well blended, then add the meat
stock or bouillon. Simmer until thick and smooth.
Add the tomato sauce, parsley and seasonings; simmer about 15 minutes. Stir in the cubed lamb and let
stand in the sauce—preferably overnight (refrigerate),
but at least an hour. Shortly before serving, sauté the
banana slices until tender in remaining 1 tablespoon
oil or butter, adding more oil or butter if necessary.
Heat the lamb mixture. Serve over Saffron Rice with
banana slices and sambals (next page).

Saffron Rice

2 1/2 cups water	1 teaspoon salt
1 cup Uncle Ben's® Converted® Rice	1/4 teaspoon saffron

75

Bring water to a boil. Add rice, salt and saffron. Cover and cook over low heat until water is absorbed, about 25 minutes.

To make a meal: Don't forget the sambals—the relishes that so enhance curry. Choose as many as you like from these: chopped peanuts, sieved hard-cooked egg, chopped green onions or chives, a good mango chutney, chopped green pepper, quartered thin slices of lemon or lime, grated coconut, chopped pineapple, watermelon pickle, mustard pickle. Serve a round loaf of bread that can be torn in chunks, and for dessert a vanilla custard poured over whatever fresh fruit is in season.

RICE WITH PESTO SAUCE   6 servings

2 cloves garlic, chopped
4 tablespoons fresh
    basil or 1 teaspoon
    dried
6 tablespoons chopped
    parsley
6 tablespoons chopped
    watercress leaves
2 tablespoons walnuts
    or pine nuts

½ cup grated Parmesan
    or Romano cheese
Olive oil, about 6
    tablespoons
3 cups hot cooked
    Uncle Ben's®
    Converted® Rice

Place garlic, basil, parsley, watercress, nuts and cheese in blender bowl. Blend at low speed until mixture is very finely chopped. Add olive oil, 2 tablespoons at a time, blending about 30 seconds after each addition until a thick, smooth sauce is formed. Season to taste with salt, pepper. Turn rice onto a hot, shallow serving dish. Spoon sauce over.

To make a meal: Contrast this highly flavored rice dish with the blandness of roasted chicken, serve sliced tomatoes with chunks of sweet pepper, Italian whole wheat bread, and a rum-flavored custard.

ARROZ VERDE

6 servings

Spanish green rice with a bonus
of chicken livers, tomato sauce

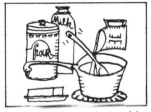

1. Bring 1¼ cups water to a boil. Add ½ cup Uncle Ben's® Converted® Rice and ½ teaspoon salt. Cover tightly and cook until all water is absorbed, about 25 minutes.

4. Combine spinach and cooked rice. Pack mixture into a ring mold. Keep warm. Sauté 1 pound chicken livers in 4 tablespoons butter. Add 1 tablespoon minced onion.

2. Meanwhile, melt 2 tablespoons butter or margarine in a saucepan. Add 2 tablespoons flour; stir until smooth. Add 1 cup milk and cook, stirring, until sauce thickens.

5. Add 1 cup whole canned tomatoes, well drained (or use 1 cup quartered fresh tomatoes). Cook over low heat until livers are done, about 20 minutes.

3. Stir in ½ cup grated sharp cheese and continue to cook, stirring, until cheese is melted and sauce is smooth. Meanwhile cook spinach, fresh or frozen, to make 1 cup.

6. Unmold rice-spinach ring onto a warm platter. Place livers in the center of the ring, spooning a little of the tomato sauce over the rice ring.

77

OEUFS POCHEES SUPREME

6 servings

A French way with poached eggs— serve for company brunch

1. Sauté ¾ cup chopped onion in 2 tablespoons butter or margarine. Add 2¼ cups chicken stock or bouillon. Stir in 1 cup Uncle Ben's® Converted® Rice.

4. Beat in 2 egg yolks and ⅓ cup grated Swiss cheese. Heat only until cheese melts. In another pan, poach 6 eggs to desired doneness.

2. Add 1 bay leaf; stir; cover. Simmer until water is absorbed, about 25 minutes. Keep warm. Melt 3 tablespoons butter in a saucepan. Add 3 tablespoons flour; stir.

5. Place rice on an ovenproof platter. Arrange eggs over rice. Spoon sauce gently over all. Place under a hot broiler until a pale golden brown. Serve at once.

3. Blend in ¼ teaspoon salt, ¼ teaspoon white pepper. Gradually stir in 1½ cups milk or light cream. Add 1 teaspoon onion juice. Stir until bubbly and thickened.

6. **To make a meal:** Serve these very special poached eggs for brunch with brown-sugar sprinkled orange slices, grilled ham, hot pecan muffins, plenty of coffee.

CASSEROLE WIZARDRY

Savory one-dish wonders

RICE BENITO
5 to 6 servings

1 large onion, thinly
    sliced
6 tablespoons butter
    or margarine
1 cup Uncle Ben's®
    Converted® Rice
2 cups chicken broth,
    hot

1 cup cooked green
    peas
1 cup cooked diced
    ham
2 tablespoons chopped
    pimiento

Sauté onion in 4 tablespoons butter or margarine until soft. Stir in rice and sauté until lightly browned. Pour in hot broth. Bake, covered, 30 to 35 minutes in 350° F. oven or until the rice is tender and the liquid is absorbed. Stir in peas, ham, 2 tablespoons butter and pimiento. Garnish with ham cut in julienne strips.

QUICK WILD RICE CASSEROLE
8 servings

2 boxes (6 ounces
    each) Uncle Ben's®
    Long Grain &
    Wild Rice
¼ cup butter or
    margarine
⅓ cup flour
1 teaspoon salt

Dash of pepper
2⅓ cups chicken broth
⅓ cup onion, finely
    chopped
⅔ cup cooked
    mushrooms
1 tablespoon parsley
    flakes

Cook rice according to package directions. Meanwhile melt 3 tablespoons butter, add flour, salt and pepper, and blend. Stirring constantly, add chicken broth gradually. Cook until thickened. Sauté onion in 1 tablespoon butter. Add mushrooms to onion. Combine cooked rice, onion, mushrooms and parsley flakes with thickened chicken broth and mix well. Pour into a baking pan. Bake in a 425° F. oven for 40 to 45 minutes.

BAKED RICE ITALIANO
4 servings

1 tablespoon butter
  or margarine
¾ cup chopped onion
½ pound Italian
  sausage (or any
  highly seasoned
  type), skinned and
  finely chopped
3 cups cooked Uncle
  Ben's® Converted®
  Rice or Quick Rice

1 cup fresh or frozen
  peas
1 can (2 ounces) sliced
  mushrooms (or
  stems and pieces),
  drained
1 can (8 ounces)
  tomato sauce
¼ cup grated
  Parmesan cheese

Brown onion and sausage lightly in melted butter or margarine. Add peas and mushrooms and stir for several minutes. Add tomato sauce; cover and simmer for 10 minutes. Combine with cooked rice and place in buttered 1-quart casserole. Sprinkle with cheese and bake in 375° F. oven for approximately 15 to 20 minutes.

To make a meal: Serve a salad-antipasto of carrot curls, cucumber fingers, crisp scallions, cubes of mild cheese, green and ripe olives, tomato wedges, all on a bed of shredded lettuce. Pass oil and vinegar. Good with all this—the very long, very thin bread sticks called grissini. Finish the meal with spumoni.

BACON CHEESE BAKE
6 servings

Put this together in the morning, bake
just before dinner time—quick and easy!

8 slices bacon
1 cup minced onion
1 cup diced celery
3 cups cooked
  Uncle Ben's®
  Converted® Rice
1 cup sliced stuffed
  olives

½ teaspoon pepper
1 can (10½ ounces)
  condensed cream
  of chicken soup
2 cups shredded
  Cheddar cheese

Left, Baked Rice Italiano

Fry bacon in a large skillet until crisp. Remove from pan. Drain well on absorbent paper; crumble into small pieces. Drain all but 3 tablespoons drippings from pan. Add onion and celery and cook until tender but not brown. Remove from heat and stir in rice, sliced olives and pepper. In a saucepan, heat chicken soup and 1 cup cheese until cheese has melted. Add sauce and bacon to the rice mixture. Turn into a greased 1½-quart casserole; top with remaining cheese. Then bake in 375° F. oven for 15 minutes.

RICE-BROCCOLI CASSEROLE   6 to 8 servings

1 box (6 ounces)
    Uncle Ben's® Long
    Grain & Wild Rice
1 package (10 ounces)
    frozen chopped
    broccoli, partially
    defrosted
1 can (10½ ounces)
    cream of
    mushroom soup

½ teaspoon salt
1 can (6½ ounces)
    chunk-style tuna,
    drained
2 eggs, separated

Cook rice as directed on package, but only 15 minutes. Break broccoli apart and spread on top of rice. Continue cooking until rice and broccoli are tender and liquid is absorbed. Remove from heat. Add soup, salt, tuna and slightly beaten egg yolks. Beat egg whites until stiff. Fold in rice mixture. Bake in 2-quart casserole 20 to 30 minutes in 350° F. oven.

Another way: Cut tops off 8 large green peppers and remove seeds. Parboil in salted water for 5 minutes; drain. Stuff with the rice mixture. Bake in a greased casserole in a 350° F. oven for 25 to 35 minutes.

Quick Trick: Leftover rice? Stir well into your favorite pancake batter, bake pancakes as usual.

GOLDEN RICE-AND-CHICKEN   6 servings

1. Cook 2 tablespoons minced onion in ¼ cup butter or margarine until soft. Stir in ½ cup flour, 1 teaspoon salt, ⅓ teaspoon pepper, ¼ teaspoon poultry seasoning.

4. Add 2 eggs, slightly beaten. to rice mixture. Fold in sauce. Butter a 10- x 6- x 2-inch baking pan and pour in rice-chicken mixture. Top with buttered crumbs.

2. Dissolve 2 chicken bouillon cubes in 1¼ cups water. Gradually add to butter mixture with ½ cup milk. Cook, stirring, until mixture bubbles and thickens.

5. Bake in 350° F. oven about 30 minutes or until set. Meanwhile sauté ½ pound mushrooms, sliced, in 2 tablespoons butter or margarine. Stir in 1 can condensed tomato soup.

3. Combine 2 cups cooked Uncle Ben's® Converted® Rice with 2 cups minced or finely diced chicken, ¼ cup chopped green pepper, ¼ cup chopped pimiento.

6. Add ¼ cup milk. Heat through. Cut baked chicken mixture into squares, top each serving with a spoonful of sauce. (Turkey may be substituted for chicken.)

83

CONTINENTAL RICE CASSEROLE   5 to 6 servings

Wine in the topping, goodies like toasted
almonds, diced apples in the casserole itself!

¼ cup minced onion
¼ cup slivered
   almonds
¼ cup butter or
   margarine
1 cup Uncle Ben's®
   Converted® Rice
2¼ cups chicken stock
   or bouillon
½ teaspoon salt
¼ teaspoon white
   pepper
1 cup cubed cooked
   chicken

1 cup cubed cooked
   beef
1 cup cubed cooked
   ham
1 medium apple,
   peeled, sliced
1 cup (4 ounces)
   grated Cheddar
   cheese
¼ cup Sauternes
1 tablespoon
   chopped green
   celery tops
   (optional)

Sauté onion and almonds in butter or margarine until
golden. Stir in rice and sauté until light brown. Add
stock or bouillon, salt and pepper. Bring to boil;
cover. Simmer 15 minutes. Stir in chicken, beef, ham
and apples. Return to boil. Cover. Simmer 10 minutes. Pour into 2½-quart casserole. Sprinkle with
cheese and wine. Bake 10 to 15 minutes in 350° F.
oven. Garnish with celery tops if desired.

WINTER CASSEROLE   4 to 5 servings

1 tablespoon chopped
   onion
1 tablespoon butter
   or margarine
2 cups Uncle Ben's®
   Quick Rice
¼ cup chopped parsley
¾ plus ¼ cup shredded
   sharp Cheddar cheese

½ teaspoon salt
1 can (10½ ounces)
   cream of
   mushroom soup
¾ cup hot water
¼ cup sliced almonds
   (optional)

Sauté onions in butter or margarine. Add rice, parsley, ¾ cup cheese, salt, soup and water. Mix well. Pour into 1½-quart greased casserole; cover. Bake in 375° F. oven until rice is tender and liquid is absorbed, about 30 minutes. Sprinkle top with remaining cheese and almonds. Broil until cheese is melted.

CHICKEN CASSEROLE   6 to 8 servings

½ cup flour
1 teaspoon salt
½ cup melted butter
   or chicken fat
2½ cups chicken stock
2 cups cooked Uncle
   Ben's® Quick Rice
2 cups cubed
   cooked chicken

1 cup fresh broiled
   mushrooms
½ cup chopped ripe
   olives
½ cup green peas
¾ cup slivered
   almonds

Stir flour and salt into butter or chicken fat in a saucepan. Stir in chicken stock. Cook until thickened, stirring constantly. Alternate layers of cooked rice, chicken, sauce and vegetables in greased 2-quart casserole. Top with slivered almonds. Bake in 350° F. oven for 30 minutes.

RICE AND HAM SCALLOP   6 to 8 servings

¾ cup Uncle Ben's®
   Converted® Rice
2 cups water
½ teaspoon salt
¼ teaspoon paprika
¼ teaspoon thyme
1 tablespoon dried
   parsley
2 tablespoons dried
   onion

1 can (10½ ounces)
   cream of chicken
   soup plus ½ soup
   can water
6 thin slices ham—⅛-
   inch thick
1 cup grated sharp
   Cheddar cheese

85

Bring water and salt to a boil in saucepan; add rice and cover tightly. Lower heat and simmer until rice is tender, about 25 minutes. Blend water gradually into soup. Meanwhile mix together paprika, thyme, parsley and onion. Cut ham into fourths, diagonally or into strips. Place half of the cooked rice on bottom of a greased 1½-quart casserole; spread one-half of seasonings, soup and ham over rice. Add remaining rice, seasonings, soup and ham. Sprinkle with the grated cheese. Cover and bake in 350° F. oven for 25 to 30 minutes.

ITALIAN BEEF CASSEROLE   6 to 8 servings

1 pound ground beef
2 tablespoons
   cooking oil
2 packages (1½
   ounces each)
   spaghetti sauce
   mix
1 can (8 ounces)
   tomato sauce
1⅓ cups water

¾ teaspoon salt
2 teaspoons lemon
   juice
Dash pepper
5 cups cooked
   Uncle Ben's®
   Converted® Rice
1⅓ cups grated
   Cheddar cheese

Brown meat in heated oil in heavy pan. Add spaghetti sauce mix, tomato sauce, water and all seasonings. Blend well. Simmer, covered, over low heat for approximately 45 minutes. Stir occasionally. Skim off any excess fat. Pour sauce over cooked rice in a buttered baking dish. Top with grated cheese. Bake, uncovered, at 325° F. for approximately 30 minutes.

To make a meal: Serve beef bouillon on the rocks with a squeeze of lemon, zucchini baked at the same time as the casserole, crusty Italian whole-wheat bread, vanilla pudding with mixed candied fruit folded into it for dessert.

FLANK ROAST WITH RICE

3 to 4 servings

The flavorsome, versatile flank
steak is the basis for this good dish

1 beef flank steak
(1¾ to 2 pounds)
1 teaspoon meat
tenderizer
1 cup minced celery
½ cup minced onion
2 tablespoons butter
or margarine

½ cup water
2 bouillon cubes
Tomato juice (optional)
1 cup uncooked
Uncle Ben's®
Converted® Rice
2 bay leaves, broken
into pieces

Tenderize steak with meat tenderizer according to
package directions. Score both sides of steak lightly.
Sprinkle with pepper. Sauté celery and onion until
tender in butter or margarine. Spread over steak and
roll lengthwise, jelly-roll fashion. Fasten with toothpicks or short skewers and lace or tie in several places
with string. Brown lightly in fat. Place with ½ cup
water in small roaster. Cover tightly and bake in 300°
F. oven for approximately 2 hours. Skim excess fat,
if present, from liquid and reserve ½ cup liquid for
later use. Dissolve bouillon cubes in remaining liquid,
measure and add sufficient water or tomato juice to
make 2¼ cups. Return liquid to pan. Stir in uncooked
rice and bay leaves. Cover tightly and continue baking for 30 minutes—or until rice and meat are tender
and liquid is absorbed. To serve, remove bay leaves
from rice and spoon rice around roast on platter.
Slice roast across the grain and pour remaining ½
cup liquid, heated, over the roast slices for extra
moistness.

To make a meal: Serve a tossed green salad, hot rolls,
Harvard beets, nut sundaes for dessert.

Above, Luncheon-in-One-Dish; below, Rice 'n' Salmon Casserole

LUNCHEON-IN-ONE-DISH

4 to 6 servings

2 cups Uncle Ben's®
  Quick Rice
1½ cups milk
  ½ teaspoon salt
  ¼ teaspoon pepper
1¼ cups grated Swiss cheese
  ¼ cup Parmesan
  cheese

1 can (10½ ounces)
  asparagus spears,
  drained
½ to 1 pound cooked
  ham, cut in strips

Combine rice, milk, salt and pepper and bring to a boil. Add ½ cup Swiss cheese and the Parmesan cheese. Cook until mixture thickens. Pour into buttered 9-inch pie plate. Arrange asparagus on top, with tips pointing toward center. Place strips of ham between. Sprinkle with remaining Swiss cheese. Cover and bake 15 minutes in 350° F. oven. Remove cover and bake until brown, about 10 minutes.

RICE 'N' SALMON CASSEROLE

4 servings

2½ cups cooked
  Uncle Ben's®
  Converted® Rice
1 can (6 to 8 ounces)
  salmon
3 tablespoons butter
  or margarine
3 tablespoons flour
¾ cup milk (or part
  salmon liquid)

½ teaspoon onion
  juice
½ teaspoon paprika
¾ teaspoon salt
⅛ teaspoon each
  pepper,
  marjoram
Dash cayenne
½ cup grated
  Cheddar cheese

Flake salmon (remove bones or crush finely) and combine with rice. Melt butter or margarine; remove from heat, blend in flour. Stir in milk and seasonings and cook over low heat until sauce is thickened. Combine sauce with rice mixture and place in 1½-quart casserole or 4 individual casseroles. Top with cheese. Cover; bake in 350° F. oven 30 minutes.

BEEF-RICE BOUNTY

8 servings

1. Combine 4 cups diced cooked roast beef with 3 cups cooked Uncle Ben's® Quick Rice. Add 2 cups sliced celery and ¾ cup chopped green pepper; stir.

3. Stir mayonnaise mixture into rice mixture. Turn into a buttered 2-quart casserole. Top with ⅔ cup crushed rice cereal. Bake in 425° F. oven for 30 minutes until heated.

2. Add ¾ cup finely chopped onion, ⅓ cup chopped pimiento. Blend 1 cup mayonnaise, ⅓ cup milk, 1 tablespoon lemon juice, 2 teaspoons salt.

4. **To make a meal:** Serve cups of lemon-laced beef bouillon, toasted cheese-topped crackers, cauliflower with brown butter, apple strudel with cheese.

ALMOND RICE FLORENTINE 4 servings

2 cups cooked Uncle
    Ben's® Rice
¼ cup blanched
    almonds, slivered
2 tablespoons butter
    or margarine
½ cup chopped onion
½ cup chopped celery
1 chicken bouillon
    cube

⅓ cup boiling water
1 can (10½ ounces)
    cream of
    mushroom soup
2 cups chopped
    cooked spinach,
    drained

Sauté almonds in butter or margarine until brown and remove from skillet. Sauté onion, celery in remaining fat. Dissolve bouillon cube in boiling water and combine with soup, using rotary beater; add onion and celery. Combine ½ of sauce with spinach and ½ with rice. Place spinach in bottom of buttered 1½-quart casserole; top with rice. Sprinkle with almonds. Bake in 350° F. oven about 40 minutes.

To make a meal: Serve sliced hard-cooked eggs with Russian dressing for an appetizer, go on to coleslaw and hot rolls and add lime ice, chocolate wafers for dessert.

CHINESE RICE CASSEROLE 8 servings

Here's a casserole to delight your
family—serve it to friends, too!

2 cups cooked
    Uncle Ben's®
    Converted® Rice
½ cup chopped green
    pepper
1 cup chopped celery

1 can (6½ ounces)
    crab meat
1 cup mayonnaise
1 cup tomato juice
¼ teaspoon salt
⅛ teaspoon pepper

½ cup finely chopped
    onion
1 can (4½ ounces)
    water chestnuts,
    drained and sliced
2 cans (4½ ounces
    each) shrimp

½ cup sliced almonds
1 tablespoon butter or
    margarine, melted
1 cup shredded
    Cheddar cheese
Paprika

Combine rice, green pepper, celery, onion, water chestnuts, seafood, mayonnaise, tomato juice and salt and pepper. Mix well. Pour into a greased 2½-quart casserole. Toast almonds in butter. Sprinkle casserole mixture with nuts, cheese and paprika. Bake in a 350° F. oven for 25 minutes.

RICE-CHEESE CASSEROLE

6 servings

3 cups cooked
    Uncle Ben's®
    Converted® Rice
4 tablespoons butter
    or margarine
4 tablespoons flour
2 cups milk
⅛ teaspoon pepper
1 teaspoon salt
Dash cayenne

½ teaspoon
    Worcestershire
    sauce
2 cups grated
    American cheese
½ cup well-buttered
    bread crumbs
Paprika
Parsley

Make white sauce: melt butter, add flour and stir until bubbly. Add milk gradually; cook, stirring, until sauce thickens and bubbles. Season with salt, pepper, cayenne and Worcestershire. Alternate layers of rice, cheese and sauce in well-greased 2-quart casserole. Sprinkle each layer lightly with paprika. Top with buttered crumbs. Bake in 350° F. oven until cheese is melted, 15 or 20 minutes. Garnish with parsley and serve piping hot.

HAM 'N' RICE BAKE

10 servings

1. Combine 2 cans (10½ ounces each) cream of celery soup with 1 cup light cream. Stir until smooth. Heat slowly until close to boiling point, but do not boil.

4. Remove sauce from heat and add cooked rice and 4 cups cubed cooked ham. Have ready 1 can (1 pound, 4 ounces) cut green beans. Butter a 3 quart casserole.

2. Stir in 1 cup grated sharp Cheddar cheese and ½ cup grated Parmesan cheese. Blend in 1½ tablespoons minced onion and 1 tablespoon prepared mustard.

5. In casserole, alternate layers of ham and rice mixture with green beans, ending with ham-and-rice mixture. Sprinkle with 1 can (3½ ounces) French fried onion rings.

3. Add 1 teaspoon grated lemon rind, ¼ teaspoon rosemary, ⅛ teaspoon pepper. While sauce is cooking, cook 4 cups Uncle Ben's® Quick Rice according to package directions.

6. Bake, uncovered, in 350° F. oven for 15 to 20 minutes or until bubbly. If your family is small, cook half, freeze half of mixture to serve at a later meal.

93

WILD RICE SUPREME
6 to 8 servings

1 package (6 ounces)
   Uncle Ben's®
   Long Grain &
   Wild Rice
¼ cup butter or
   margarine
⅓ cup chopped onion
⅓ cup all-purpose flour
1 teaspoon salt
Pepper to taste

1 cup half-and-half
1 cup chicken broth
2 cups cooked cubed
   chicken
⅓ cup chopped
   pimiento
⅓ cup chopped parsley
3 tablespoons
   chopped blanched
   almonds

Cook rice according to package directions. Sauté the onions in butter. Add flour, salt, pepper, and blend. Stirring constantly, gradually add half-and-half and chicken broth. Cook until thickened. Add sauce, chicken, pimiento, parsley and almonds to cooked rice and mix well. Pour into a greased baking pan. Bake in 425° F. oven for 30 minutes.

SPANISH PORK CHOPS
4 servings

2 cups cooked
   Uncle Ben's®
   Converted® Rice
4 lean pork chops
1 tablespoon fat
¼ cup diced onion
⅓ cup diced celery
2 tablespoons diced
   green pepper

1½ cups canned
   tomatoes
1½ teaspoons salt
¼ teaspoon pepper
2 tablespoons
   minced parsley

Brown chops in heavy skillet. Remove chops and add onion, celery and green pepper to drippings. Sauté until tender. Add tomatoes, salt, pepper. Simmer 10 minutes. Place chops in baking dish and sprinkle with salt and pepper. Top each with mound of ½ cup cooked rice. Pour sauce over all and sprinkle with parsley. Cover and bake at 350° F. for approximately 1 hour. Just before serving, spoon sauce over chops.

Above, Wild Rice Supreme; below, Spanish Pork Chops

CRAB-RICE BAKE

6 servings

1 cup Uncle Ben's®
   Converted® Rice
1 envelope chicken-
   noodle soup mix
1 tablespoon butter
   or margarine
1 teaspoon salt
3½ cups water
2 cans (6½ ounces
   each) crab meat

1 teaspoon prepared
   mustard
1 teaspoon lemon
   juice
1 medium tomato,
   sliced
½ cup finely grated
   Cheddar cheese

Combine rice, soup mix, margarine, salt and water in a saucepan. Bring to a boil, cover and simmer until rice is tender, about 25 minutes. Drain and remove any shell or cartilage from crab meat. Combine crab meat, mustard and lemon juice with rice mixture. Spoon into a shallow casserole or individual casseroles. Top with tomato slices and grated cheese. Broil until cheese melts and browns lightly.

CHICKEN CASSEROLE WITH WILD RICE

4 to 6 servings

1 box (6 ounces)
   Uncle Ben's® Long
   Grain & Wild Rice
2 cups hot water
1 fryer chicken, cut up
Salt, black pepper
½ cup milk

1 can (10½ ounces)
   cream of
   mushroom soup
½ cup slivered
   almonds
1 tablespoon butter
   or margarine

Combine contents of rice package with water in 2½-quart casserole. Salt and pepper chicken to taste. Arrange on top of rice mixture. Bake, covered, in 375° F. oven, 1¼ hours or until chicken is done. Combine milk and soup. Sauté almonds in butter or margarine. When casserole is done, pour soup mixture over casserole. Sprinkle top with almonds. Return to oven, uncovered, and bake until soup is bubbly, casserole heated through.

SOMETHING SPECIAL

Browse here for unusual recipes

CHINESE FRIED RICE
4 to 6 servings

2 small pork chops
2 tablespoons fat
⅔ cup chopped onion
1 cup Uncle Ben's®
   Converted® Rice

1 egg, beaten
   (optional)

Remove meat from chop bones and dice. Brown in fat in a skillet. Meanwhile, cook rice according to package directions. Remove meat from pan and brown onions in remaining fat. Return pork to pan and add cooked rice. Toss lightly until brown. Add egg, if desired, and cook briefly. Serve in individual bowls. Garnish, if desired, with chopped green onions.

QUICK-FRIED RICE
4 to 5 servings

2 tablespoons
   chopped onion
2 tablespoons butter
   or margarine
2 cups Uncle Ben's®
   Quick Rice
1⅔ cups water
2 beef bouillon cubes

½ teaspoon salt
Dash pepper
2 eggs, slightly
   beaten
¼ cup chopped green
   onions with tops
2 teaspoons soy sauce

Sauté onion in butter until transparent but not browned. Add rice, water, bouillon cubes, salt and pepper. Bring to a vigorous boil. Cover and cook over low heat until all water is absorbed, about 5 minutes. Stir in eggs and green onions. Cook until eggs are set. Stir in soy sauce.

97

Above, Cheese and Rice Soufflé; below, Red Beans and Rice

CHEESE AND RICE SOUFFLE

5 to 6 servings

*Only one warning about this easy, puffy wonder—
as with all soufflés, serve the moment it's done*

2 tablespoons butter or margarine	4 eggs, separated
3 tablespoons flour	½ teaspoon salt
¾ cup milk	Dash cayenne
½ pound sharp cheese, grated	1 cup cooked Uncle Ben's® Converted® Rice

Combine butter and flour in a saucepan, stir over low heat until smooth. Gradually add milk; cook, stirring, until thickened. Add cheese, salt and cayenne; cook, stirring occasionally, until thick. Beat egg yolks lightly with a fork. Add slowly to cooking mixture, stirring constantly. Remove from heat and stir in rice. Beat egg whites until stiff but not dry. Gently fold in cheese-rice mixture. Turn into a greased 1½-quart casserole. Bake, uncovered, in a 325° F. oven for 40 minutes. Then serve at once.

RED BEANS AND RICE

6 servings

1 pound red beans (kidney or other)	1 tablespoon minced parsley (if desired)
½ pound salt pork, sliced	1 cup uncooked Uncle Ben's® Converted® Rice
1 small onion, sliced	
Salt, pepper to taste	
Garlic and Tabasco or chili powder (if desired)	

Pick through and wash beans. Cover with water, add pork, and simmer. After 1 hour of cooking, add onion and seasonings to taste. Continue cooking until beans are tender, adding water as necessary. Meanwhile, cook rice according to package directions. Serve beans over cooked rice.

99

BUSY-DAY DINNER   4 servings

For a peppier flavor, add a little chili
sauce or Worcestershire to this dish

2 tablespoons
  minced onion
1 tablespoon butter
  or margarine
1½ cups chopped left-
  over (or canned)
  meat—ham,
  chicken, sausage,
  beef

3 cups cooked
  Uncle Ben's®
  Converted® Rice
1 can (10½ ounces)
  cream of
  mushroom soup
Salt, if needed
Grated cheese
  (optional)

Sauté onion in butter or margarine in skillet until tender. Add meat, cooked rice, cream of mushroom
soup and salt, if needed. If extra moistness is desired,
add small amount of water or milk. Cover and simmer over very low heat about 20 minutes. Serve from
a skillet—or turn onto a warm platter—and sprinkle
with grated cheese if desired.

To make a meal: Serve with a tossed green salad (add
any leftover cooked vegetables the refrigerator may
harbor) garlic bread, apples—or other fruit—with
cheese wedges for dessert.

NEW ORLEANS RICE STUFFING   about 11 cups

You'll like this so much you'll want to serve
it as a side dish even when there's no bird to stuff

2 cups Uncle Ben's®
  Converted® Rice
3 large onions, finely
  chopped
4 large stalks of celery,
  finely chopped
1 green pepper, chopped
Turkey heart, gizzard
  and liver, ground

Turkey fat, finely
  chopped
⅔ cup chopped parsley
1 cup chopped pecans
2 whole eggs, well
  beaten
Salt, pepper, poultry
  seasoning to taste

Cook rice according to package directions. While the rice is cooking, sauté vegetables, liver, gizzard and heart together with rendered or chopped turkey fat in skillet. Cook thoroughly. Add seasonings, stir to blend. Turn off heat under skillet; add rice and fold in eggs, mixing thoroughly. Add chopped nuts and chopped parsley. Remove from skillet, stuff turkey and bake until done.

Other ways: Oysters may be added to this stuffing, if desired. Or vary it sometimes with cooked fresh or canned mushrooms.

TOASTED RICE STUFFING   about 12 cups

2 cups Uncle Ben's®
   Converted® Rice
2 cups each chopped
   onion, celery,
   green pepper
2 teaspoons salt
5 cups stock or
   bouillon

2 eggs, well beaten
1 teaspoon poultry
   seasoning
½ cup minced parsley
   or celery tops

Spread uncooked rice in a shallow pan. Toast in a 350° F. oven for approximately 15 to 20 minutes or until kernels are golden brown. Stir rice or shake pan occasionally for even browning. Place onion, celery, green pepper and salt in stock or bouillon. Bring to boil. Stir in toasted rice. Turn heat low and cover. Cook approximately 25 minutes or until liquid is absorbed and rice is tender. Remove from heat. Fold in eggs, poultry seasoning and minced parsley or celery tops. Taste and add more seasonings if needed. Stuff fowl with mixture and bake.

Other ways: For variety, add any or all of the following: 1 cup or more button or sliced mushrooms, toasted slivered almonds, chopped pecans.

101

BEST-EVER WILD RICE DRESSING

4 to 5 servings

1 box (6 ounces)
    Uncle Ben's® Long
    Grain & Wild Rice
2 tablespoons butter
    or margarine
Finely grated rind of 1
    medium orange

Juice of 1 medium
    orange plus water
    to equal 2½ cups
½ cup pecans,
    chopped

Sauté rice in packet in butter or margarine until brown, stirring frequently. Stir in contents of seasoning packet, orange rind, orange juice and water. Bring to boil; cover. Simmer until liquid is absorbed, about 25 minutes. Stir in pecans.

You'll want to know: Serve as accompaniment to chicken or use to stuff Cornish game hens. Garnish with green seedless grapes and mandarin orange sections.

RICE STUFFING —MEAT, FISH OR FOWL

3 cups

Try this stuffing in a whole red
snapper for a handsome company dish

2 tablespoons chopped
    onion
1 cup diced celery
2 tablespoons fat
2 cups cooked Uncle
    Ben's®
    Converted® Rice

1 teaspoon chopped
    parsley
Salt, pepper
2 teaspoons
    Worcestershire
    sauce

Brown onion and celery in fat. Add rice, parsley, salt, pepper and Worcestershire sauce.

Other ways: Add 2 hard-cooked eggs, diced, or 3 tablespoons cooked chopped bacon, or ½ pint oysters, or ½ cup sautéed mushrooms.

Right, Best-Ever Wild Rice Dressing

TUNA-RICE PUFF

6 servings

1. Melt ⅓ cup butter or margarine. Add ¼ cup flour, 1 teaspoon salt, ¼ teaspoon pepper. Gradually add 1½ cups of milk. Cook, stirring.

4. Beat 2 egg whites until stiff but not dry. Fold into mixture. Pour mixture into ungreased 1½-quart casserole. Cut 3 slices process American cheese in half, diagonally.

2. Beat 2 egg yolks slightly. Stir a little of this hot sauce into yolks, then add yolks to cooking sauce and mix thoroughly. Cook 2 minutes longer, stirring constantly.

5. Arrange cheese slices around edge of casserole in an attractive pattern. Set casserole in a pan of hot water. Bake in 350° F. oven about 40 minutes or until firm.

3. Remove from heat. Fold in 1 can (7 ounces) tuna, flaked; add 2 tablespoons grated onion, 1 tablespoon lemon juice, 2 cups cooked Uncle Ben's® Converted® Rice.

6. To make a meal: Serve with frosty tomato juice to start, sautéed zucchini and yellow squash, rye bread, fresh strawberry-rhubarb tarts for dessert.

FARMER'S OMELET   4 servings

Garnish with tart currant jelly, serve
for a special brunch, a satisfying supper

2 tablespoons butter   2 tablespoons chopped
   or margarine   chives
2 cups cooked, hot   4 eggs
   Uncle Ben's®   2 tablespoons cream
   Converted® Rice   Salt, white pepper

Melt butter in a skillet. Add rice, chives. Beat the
eggs and cream together lightly. Season with salt and
pepper; pour over rice. Cook over low heat, stirring
and turning, until the eggs are set.

To make a meal: For brunch serve this omelet with
chilled orange juice, grilled Canadian bacon, hot biscuits or popovers (made from scratch or from a mix)
with lime marmalade, plenty of hot coffee.

RICE AND MUSHROOM DRESSING   6 servings

1 package (6 ounces)   5 tablespoons butter
   Uncle Ben's® Long   or margarine
   Grain & Wild Rice   ¼ teaspoon poultry
1 cup chopped celery   seasoning
1 cup (approximately   (optional)
   2 4-ounce cans)   Water
   sliced mushrooms   2 eggs, beaten slightly
   or mushroom   1 cup dry bread
   pieces (drain,   crumbs or crushed
   reserve liquid)   soda crackers

Sauté uncooked rice (set aside seasoning envelope
for later use), celery and mushrooms in 1 tablespoon
melted butter or margarine until rice is lightly
browned. Stir occasionally. Add seasonings from en-

velope, and poultry seasoning. Measure mushroom liquid plus water to make 2½ cups; add to rice. Cover and bring to a boil; cook over low heat until all water is absorbed, about 25 minutes. Remove from heat. Blend in eggs. Stir in bread crumbs or crackers and 4 tablespoons melted butter or margarine.

You'll want to know: Makes a delicious stuffing for roasting chicken or small turkey. Also may be baked separately in a 1½-quart casserole. Add 1 cup bouillon to make dressing more moist and bake, covered, in 350° F. oven for 20 to 25 minutes.

WILD RICE OMELET   4 to 6 servings

Wild rice lends never-before flavor
to make an omelet into a masterpiece

1 package (6 ounces)
Uncle Ben's® Long
Grain & Wild Rice
4 eggs, separated
½ teaspoon salt

⅛ teaspoon pepper
2 tablespoons hot
water
1 tablespoon butter or
margarine, melted

Cook rice as directed on package. Beat egg yolks until thick and lemon-colored. Add salt, pepper, water, melted butter or margarine and cooked rice. Beat egg whites until they form peaks. Carefully fold rice mixture into egg whites. Cook in large, well-buttered skillet or omelet pan. Fold and turn onto hot platter. Serve with tomato or cheese sauce, or sour cream and crumbled bacon.

To make a meal: For a hearty Sunday brunch, serve this dish with broiled grapefruit halves, hot date muffins, broiled bacon strips, plenty of coffee—cocoa for the children.

RICE PIZZA

5 to 6 servings

"Best pizza ever" the youngsters say—
and who knows better than those experts?

¼ cup chopped onion
1 tablespoon cooking
   oil
1 can (8 ounces)
   tomato sauce
1¾ cups water
1½ teaspoons salt
Garlic seasoning,
   oregano or basil,
   pepper and
   sugar (to taste)

¾ cup Uncle Ben's®
   Converted® Rice
Pepperoni, mushrooms
   and/or anchovies
3 to 6 ounces
   Mozzarella
   cheese, sliced
⅓ to ½ cup grated
   Parmesan cheese

Sauté onion in oil; remove from heat. Add tomato sauce, water, salt and other seasonings to taste. Add rice. Bring to a boil. Stir well. Cover and lower heat. Cook 20 to 25 minutes or until rice is tender and sauce is cooked down thick. Stir to prevent sticking; add a bit of water if needed. Turn mixture into a well-oiled pizza pan or 2 pie pans. Spread, making a slight rim. Arrange pepperoni, mushrooms and/or anchovies over top. Cover with cheese slices. Sprinkle with Parmesan. Slip under broiler to brown. Cut in wedges. Serve on plates.

You'll want to know: A simpler version of this dish is delicious, too—omit pepperoni, etc. Cover rice "crust" with cheese only.

Quick Trick: Leftover rice? Warm it gently in a little butter or margarine with whatever leftover vegetables your refrigerator has to offer. If there's a dab of leftover fish, chicken or meat, add that, too. Lunch is served!

GOLDEN RICE LOAF

6 to 8 servings

1. Combine 3 cups Uncle Ben's® Quick Rice, 2¼ cups water, ¾ teaspoon salt in a saucepan. Stir; bring to a boil. Cover ; simmer 5 minutes.

2. In another saucepan, combine ⅓ cup flour, 1¼ teaspoons salt, ⅛ teaspoon pepper, ½ teaspoon dry mustard, ¼ teaspoon sage, ½ cup milk.

3. Mix well. Add 1½ cups milk and cook until thickened, stirring frequently. Add 2 cups grated sharp Cheddar cheese and stir until melted.

4. Hard-cook 3 eggs. Remove cheese sauce from heat. Fold in cooked rice, 1 tablespoon grated onion. Beat 3 eggs slightly. Stir eggs into rice mixture.

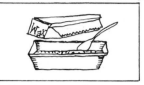

5. Line bottom of a greased loaf pan with waxed paper. Shell hard-cooked eggs. Place half of rice-cheese mixture in bottom of the loaf pan.

6. Arrange the hard-cooked eggs lengthwise down the center. Cover with remaining rice-cheese mixture. Place loaf pan in another pan containing hot water.

7. Bake in 350° F. oven about 1 hour or until set. Let loaf "rest" about 5 minutes after taking out of oven. Turn out of pan; slice and serve.

8. If desired, serve with a well-seasoned tomato sauce or with a medium white sauce to which sautéed chopped mushrooms and a little dill have been added.

HOT, COLD—WONDERFUL

A whole new world of rice salads

SKILLET SALAD

6 to 8 servings

1 box (6 ounces)
Uncle Ben's®
Long Grain &
Wild Rice
3 tablespoons bacon
drippings
1 tablespoon flour
1½ teaspoons salt
1 tablespoon sugar
¾ cup water
¼ cup vinegar
1 small head romaine,
about 4 cups
(packed) when
broken into bite-
size pieces

1 cup ½-inch pieces
celery
1 small onion, sliced
and separated
into rings
½ cup sliced radishes
1 cup sliced
cucumbers
6 slices crisp-fried
bacon, broken
into bite-size
pieces

Cook contents of rice package as directed in 12-inch skillet. When rice is tender, move to side of pan. Pour in bacon drippings. Blend in flour, salt and sugar. Add water and vinegar. Cook over low heat until sauce is smooth. Remove pan from heat. Add vegetables and bacon. Toss with rice until all ingredients are coated with sauce. Serve hot.

ZESTY CHICKEN SALAD

4 to 6 servings

¾ cup mayonnaise
2 tablespoons lemon
juice
1½ cups cubed cooked
chicken
1 cup cold cooked
Uncle Ben's®
Converted® Rice

½ cup chopped celery
2 tablespoons grated
onion
½ cup chopped
cucumber pickle
¼ cup diced ripe
pitted olives

Mix mayonnaise and lemon juice. Combine other ingredients. Toss with mayonnaise-lemon mixture.

109

RICE AND SHRIMP SALAD   6 to 8 servings

Cool and pretty, this salad will
make a summer meal something special

2 cups cooked
  Uncle Ben's®
  Converted® Rice,
  cooled
2 cups cooked
  shrimp, halved
  lengthwise
1 cup celery, thinly
  sliced crosswise
⅔ cup thin julienne
  strips green
  pepper
1 can (13½ ounces)
  pineapple tidbits,
  drained

Dressing:
3 tablespoons vinegar
1½ tablespoons salad
  oil
1 teaspoon
  Worcestershire
  sauce
1 teaspoon sugar
½ teaspoon salt
½ teaspoon curry
  powder
⅛ teaspoon ginger
  powder
Dash black pepper

Combine rice, shrimp, celery, green peppers and
pineapple. Combine remaining ingredients to form
dressing. Pour over rice mixture and stir. Let chill and
marinate at least three hours. Serve garnished with
more shrimp, watercress sprigs.

RICE AND TUNA MEDLEY   4 servings

2 cups cold cooked
  Uncle Ben's®
  Converted® Rice
1 can (6½ ounces)
  chunk-style tuna
¾ cup cooked green
  peas
¼ cup chopped pickles

⅓ cup chopped celery
2 tablespoons
  chopped pimiento
  (if desired)
Salt, pepper to taste
Salad dressing, as
  desired

Combine all ingredients and toss lightly. Serve with
favorite dressing. Garnish with tomato quarters,
olives or celery curls.

Right, Rice and Shrimp Salad

GOURMET WILD RICE SALAD   4 to 6 servings

1 package (6 ounces)
Uncle Ben's® Long
Grain & Wild Rice
¼ cup canned
artichoke hearts,
drained and cut in
bite-size pieces

¼ cup cold cooked
green peas
6 cherry tomatoes,
halved
2 green onions and
tops, chopped
¼ cup French dressing

Cook contents of rice package as directed. Cool cooked rice slightly and add all remaining ingredients. Toss salad lightly. Serve at room temperature.

To make a meal: For a party, serve with cold sliced turkey (smoked turkey if you're really being elegant) and ham, spears of endive stuffed with chive cheese, hot rolls, frozen éclairs with caramel sauce.

IMPERIAL SALAD   6 servings

4 cups Uncle Ben's®
Quick Rice
3 tomatoes, cut in thin
strips
1 green pepper, cut in
strips
¼ cup slivered
pimiento
4 scallions, very finely
sliced

1 can (8 ounces) peas
1 can (4 ounces) black
olives, chopped
3 tablespoons wine
vinegar
1 teaspoon dry
mustard
Salt, pepper
1 clove garlic, mashed

Cook rice according to package directions. Combine remaining ingredients; toss with rice to mix. Chill before serving; mound on platter. Garnish with watercress, tomato strips, black olives, cucumber slices, if desired.

To make a meal: For a hot-weather company dinner serve this with king crab cocktail, cold Vitello Tonnato, salt sticks, chocolate mousse for dessert.

Above, Gourmet Wild Rice Salad; below, Imperial Salad

Above, Come-to-Lunch Salad; below, Easy Rice-Fruit Salad

COME-TO-LUNCH SALAD   4 servings

1½ cups cooked
    Uncle Ben's®
    Converted® Rice
2 hard-cooked eggs
    (chopped)
¼ cup ground pickles
    (sour or dill)
¼ cup sweet pickles
½ cup diced cold
    chicken

¼ cup diced celery
¼ cup diced onions
2 pimientos, diced
⅛ teaspoon paprika
½ teaspoon salt
1 tablespoon pre-
    pared mustard
⅓ cup mayonnaise

Combine all ingredients; chill. Garnish with tomato wedges and endive.

To make a meal: Serve to luncheon guests with cups of jellied madrilène with lemon wedges; heated, buttered rusks; orange ice with crème de menthe topping. If you prefer, use flaked tuna in the salad in place of chicken.

EASY RICE-FRUIT SALAD   6 servings

2 cups Uncle Ben's®
    Quick Rice
¼ cup pecans, broken
1 banana, cut into
    ½-inch pieces
½ cup pineapple cubes
1 orange, peeled and
    sectioned

1 apple, cut into
    ½-inch pieces
Maraschino cherries
    (with stems) for
    garnish

Cook rice as directed on package. Set pan of rice in cold tap water to cool quickly. Combine with pecans and fruit (except cherries). Mound individual servings on crisp lettuce leaves. Garnish just before serving with maraschino cherries. Top each serving with Orange Cream Dressing (page 116).

115

Orange Cream Dressing

⅓ cup orange juice
2 teaspoons lemon
    juice
¼ cup sugar

½ teaspoon salt
2 egg yolks
½ cup whipping cream

Combine first four ingredients in a saucepan. Bring to a boil on high heat. Cool slightly; add egg yolks, one at a time, beating well after each addition. Cook over low heat until mixture thickens, stirring occasionally. Cool. Fold in whipped cream.

WILD RICE CHICKEN SALAD MOLD

8 servings

1 package (6 ounces)
    Uncle Ben's® Long
    Grain & Wild Rice
2 cups cooked
    chicken, boned,
    diced
⅔ cup chopped green
    pepper
¾ cup diced celery
⅓ cup (2-ounce jar)
    chopped pimiento
2 hard-cooked eggs,
    diced

1 tablespoon
    (1 envelope)
    unflavored gelatin
1 cup chicken broth
2 teaspoons salt
1 tablespoon lemon
    juice
⅓ cup mayonnaise
⅓ cup creamy French
    dressing

Cook rice as directed on package. Combine cooked rice mixture, diced chicken, green pepper, celery, pimiento and hard-cooked eggs. Soak gelatin in chicken broth until soft; heat and stir until gelatin is completely dissolved. Combine gelatin solution, salt, lemon juice, mayonnaise, French dressing and add to the salad ingredients. Mix well. Pour into salad mold. Chill and allow to set until firm (about 1 hour) before serving. Garnish with parsley or salad greens, tomato wedges and/or stuffed olives.

SWEET AND SAVORY

Happy-endings rice desserts

MOCHA RICE PUDDING

4 servings

⅓ cup Uncle Ben's®
    Converted® Rice
1½ cups strong coffee
1 tablespoon butter
    or margarine
2 eggs, well beaten

1 cup milk
⅓ cup dark corn syrup
⅓ cup sugar
½ teaspoon vanilla
⅛ teaspoon salt
Cinnamon

Place uncooked rice in coffee in double boiler. Cook approximately 35 minutes or until rice is tender. Add butter or margarine and combine thoroughly with remaining ingredients. Pour into buttered 1-quart baking dish. Sprinkle with cinnamon and set in pan of warm water. Bake in 350° F. oven for about 50 minutes or until knife inserted in center comes out clean. Serve warm or cold, with whipped or light cream

LEMON RICE PUDDING

6 servings

1 cup Uncle Ben's®
    Quick Rice
1⅔ cups cold water
¼ teaspoon salt
½ teaspoon butter
    or margarine
1⅓ cups milk

⅓ cup sugar
1¼ teaspoons
    cornstarch
2 egg yolks, beaten
1 teaspoon grated
    lemon rind

Bring rice, cold water, salt and butter to a boil in a saucepan. Stir; boil rapidly until most of the liquid is absorbed, 7 to 10 minutes. Mix milk, sugar and cornstarch; add to rice. Cool, stirring, 3 minutes. Remove from heat. Slowly stir in beaten egg yolks and lemon rind. Heat to boiling. Chill the pudding, or serve it warm.

RICE CHEESECAKE

6 to 8 servings

1½ cups Uncle Ben's®
   Quick Rice
1⅓ cups water
1 tablespoon butter
   or margarine
⅓ teaspoon salt
1½ cups graham-
   cracker crumbs
   (about 18
   crackers)
½ cup brown sugar

½ teaspoon cinnamon
½ cup melted butter
   or margarine
2 cups creamed
   cottage cheese
½ cup milk
1 package instant
   lemon pudding
   mix
½ cup sour cream or
   cherry preserves

Combine rice, water, butter or margarine and salt; cook as directed on package. Cool to room temperature. Mix graham-cracker crumbs with brown sugar, cinnamon and butter or margarine. With the back of a spoon, press mixture into bottom and ½-inch-up sides of a buttered 9-inch-square cake pan or spring-form mold. Chill. Press cottage cheese through a coarse sieve or whip until fairly smooth. Combine with milk and pudding mix and beat about 1 minute. Fold in rice and pour into cooled crumb crust. Chill 1 hour. Before serving, top with sour cream and/or peaches or other fruit.

RIZ A L'IMPERATRICE

6 servings

½ cup Uncle Ben's®
   Converted® Rice
1¼ cups milk
4 egg yolks
½ cup sugar
¾ cup hot milk
Small piece vanilla bean

1 envelope gelatin
2 tablespoons cold
   water
¾ cup finely chopped
   candied fruits
1 cup heavy cream,
   whipped

Cook rice in milk in top of double boiler. Pour in mixing bowl. Now combine beaten egg yolks, sugar, hot milk and vanilla bean in the top of the double boiler. Cook over boiling water, stirring constantly

Above, Rice Cheesecake; below, Riz à l'Imperatrice

until thick and smooth. Stir in 1 envelope gelatin softened in 2 tablespoons water. Add rice, candied fruits and 1 cup heavy cream, whipped. Turn rice into a decorative ring mold and chill in the refrigerator for at least 4 hours. To serve, unmold the rice onto a chilled platter and garnish it attractively with fresh strawberries and leaves. The mold may be surrounded at the base by red currant jelly, melted and diluted with a little kirsch and whipped to smoothness.

BAVARIAN RICE

8 servings

A make-ahead beauty of a dessert to
grace any company-for-dinner occasion

1 envelope
(1 tablespoon)
unflavored
gelatin
¼ cup cold water
¼ cup hot water
2 cups milk
2 cups Uncle Ben's® Quick Rice

½ cup sugar
¼ teaspoon salt
1¼ teaspoons vanilla
1 cup whipping cream
1 cup apricot jam or preserves
Maraschino cherries

Soften gelatin in cold water, then dissolve in hot water. Bring milk and rice to a boil and cook 5 minutes. Cover and set aside 5 minutes. Add sugar, salt, vanilla and gelatin. Mix well and chill until slightly thickened. Whip cream until stiff and fold into rice mixture. Pour into 1-quart mold and chill for 2 hours. To serve, unmold on large plate and cover thickly with jam or preserves. Garnish with maraschino cherries.

Other ways: If apricot jam is not your cup of tea, use cherry preserves, or strawberry, or any flavor that is a particular favorite in your house.

Right, Bavarian Rice

Above, Cherry Rice Dessert; below, Pineapple-Rice Mallow

CHERRY RICE DESSERT
6 servings

2 cups Uncle Ben's®
  Quick Rice
2 cups water
½ teaspoon salt
1 teaspoon butter
  or margarine
1 can (20 ounces) sour
  cherries, well
  drained (reserve
  juice)

½ cup sugar
½ teaspoon vanilla (or
  almond) extract
½ cup whipping cream
Sauce:
½ cup sugar
1 tablespoon cornstarch
Dash salt
Cherry juice and water
  to make 1 cup

Combine rice, water, salt and butter in a large sauce-pan. Bring to a boil, lower heat and cover. Cook until all liquid is absorbed. Remove from heat and set in a pan of cold tap water to cool quickly, about 15 min-utes. Prepare sauce by blending sugar, cornstarch and salt. Gradually add liquid. Cook over medium heat until clear, stirring constantly; cool. Combine cooled rice with cherries, sugar and vanilla. Lightly fold in cream which has been beaten stiff. Serve im-mediately in sherbet glasses with cooled cherry sauce.

PINEAPPLE-RICE MALLOW
12 servings

2 cups cooked
  Uncle Ben's®
  Converted® Rice
1 cup water
1 cup pineapple juice
  (drained from
  pineapple
  canned in extra
  heavy syrup)
¼ pound
  marshmallows

(miniature or, if
  large, cut in
  quarters)
1½ to 2 cups canned
  pineapple tidbits
  and maraschino
  cherries, cut and
  well drained
Juice of ½ lemon
1 cup (½ pint) heavy
  cream, whipped

Combine rice, water and ½ cup of pineapple juice in a pan large enough to allow for some "foaming."

Bring to a boil; cover, lower heat and simmer until most of the liquid is absorbed, about 15 minutes. Remove from heat and add ½ cup pineapple juice and marshmallows, folding only until marshmallows are half melted. Chill and cool until partially set. Then fold in fruit, lemon juice and whipped cream. Pile mixture into individual serving dishes, or one large one, and chill at least 3 hours or until set. Garnish with sliced fruit or berries, or with grated coconut, or with toasted almonds, or any combination.

OLD-FASHIONED BAKED CUSTARD 4 servings

"Like mother used to make" describes
this good, brings-back-memories pudding

½ cup Uncle Ben's®	2 eggs, beaten
Converted® Rice	⅓ cup sugar
1 teaspoon salt	Pinch salt
1¾ cups water	1 teaspoon vanilla
2 cups milk	Nutmeg or cinnamon

Stir rice and salt into boiling water in 3-quart saucepan. Cover tightly and cook over low heat until water is absorbed, about 28 to 30 minutes. Add milk and cook gently, stirring occasionally, until mixture is creamy—about 5 minutes. Combine eggs, sugar, salt and vanilla. Slowly stir rice mixture into egg mixture. Pour into greased 1½-quart casserole. Sprinkle with nutmeg or cinnamon if desired. Place in pan containing 1 inch hot water. Bake in 350° F. oven 45 to 50 minutes or until a knife inserted comes out clean. Serve warm or chilled, plain or with cream.

To make a meal: Let this good dessert be the finishing touch of an old-time meal of baked ham, candied sweet potatoes, new peas and tiny onions, and corn sticks.

INDEX